Second Workshop on Applying Machine Learning Techniques to Optimise the Division of Labour in Hybrid MT

(ML4HMT-2012)

Held at the 24th International Conference on Computational Linguistics (COLING 2012)

Mumbai, India
15 December 2012

Editors:

Josef Van Genabith
Toni Badia
Christian Federmann
Maite Melero
Marta R. Costa-jussa
Tsuyoshi Okita

ISBN: 978-1-62748-357-5

Printed from e-media with permission by:

Curran Associates, Inc.
57 Morehouse Lane
Red Hook, NY 12571

Some format issues inherent in the e-media version may also appear in this print version.

Printed by Curran Associates, Inc. (2013)

Association for Computational Linguistics
209 N. Eighth Street
Stroudsburg, Pennsylvania 18360

Phone: 1-570-476-8006
Fax: 1-570-476-0860

acl@aclweb.org

Additional copies of this publication are available from:

Curran Associates, Inc.
57 Morehouse Lane
Red Hook, NY 12571 USA
Phone: 845-758-0400
Fax: 845-758-2634
Email: curran@proceedings.com
Web: www.proceedings.com

COLING 2012

24th International Conference on Computational Linguistics

Proceedings of the Second Workshop on Applying Machine Learning Techniques to Optimise the Division of Labour in Hybrid MT

Workshop chairs:

Josef van Genabith, Toni Badia, Christian Federmann,
Maite Melero, Marta R. Costa-jussà and Tsuyoshi Okita

Diamond sponsors

Tata Consultancy Services
Linguistic Data Consortium for Indian Languages (LDC-IL)

Gold Sponsors

Microsoft Research
Beijing Baidu Netcon Science Technology Co. Ltd.

Silver sponsors

IBM, India Private Limited
Crimson Interactive Pvt. Ltd.
Yahoo
Easy Transcription & Software Pvt. Ltd.

Message from the Workshop organisers

We are delighted to welcome you to the of the Second Workshop on Applying Machine Learning Techniques to Optimise the Division of Labour in Hybrid MT and associated Shared Task (ML4HMT-2012) in Mumbai.

The Shared Task is an effort to trigger systematic investigation on improving state-of-the-art Hybrid MT, using advanced machine-learning (ML) methodologies. Its main focus is trying to answer the following question: *Can Hybrid/System Combination MT techniques benefit from extra information (linguistically motivated, decoding and runtime) from the different systems involved?*

Participants to the challenge are requested to build hybrid translations by combining the output of several MT systems of different types. Five participating combination systems, each following a different solution strategy, have been submitted to the shared task.

The Workshop will be composed of two parts. In the first part we will have an invited talk and the presentation of three research papers. In the second part, participants to the shared task will describe their systems and results. At the end of this part, there will be a presentation of the joint evaluation, followed by a discussion panel.

We are looking forward to an interesting workshop and want to thank all authors, presenters and attendees for making this a successful workshop.

Acknowledgments

This work has been funded under the Seventh Framework Programme for Research and Technological Development of the European Commission through the T4ME contract (grant agreement no.:249119).

We thank the organisers of COLING 2012 for their support.

Organisation committee

Prof. Josef van Genabith, Dublin City University (DCU) and Centre for Next Generation Localisation (CNGL)

Prof. Toni Badia, Universitat Pompeu Fabra and Barcelona Media (BM)

Christian Federmann, German Research Center for Artificial Intelligence (DFKI), contact person: cfedermann@dfki.de

Dr. Maite Melero, Barcelona Media (BM)

Dr. Marta R. Costa-jussà, Barcelona Media (BM)

Dr. Tsuyoshi Okita, Dublin City University (DCU)

The ML4HMT-2012 workshop is supported by META-NET

Organizers:

Prof. Josef van Genabith (Dublin City University (DCU) and Centre for Next Generation Localisation (CNGL))
Prof. Toni Badia (Universitat Pompeu Fabra and Barcelona Media (BM))
Christian Federmann (German Research Center for Artificial Intelligence (DFKI))
Dr. Maite Melero (Barcelona Media (BM))
Dr. Marta R. Costa-jussà (Barcelona Media (BM))
Dr. Tsuyoshi Okita (Dublin City University (DCU))

Programme Committee:

Eleftherios Avramidis (German Research Center for Artificial Intelligence, Germany)
Prof. Sivaji Bandyopadhyay (Jadavpur University, India)
Dr. Rafael Banchs (Institute for Infocomm Research I2R, Singapore)
Prof. Loïc Barrault (LIUM University of Le Mans, France)
Prof. Antal van den Bosch (Centre for Language Studies, Radboud University Nijmegen, Netherlands)
Dr. Grzegorz Chrupala (Saarland University, Saarbrücken, Germany)
Prof. Jinhua Du (Xi'an University of Technology (XAUT), China)
Dr. Andreas Eisele (DirectorateGeneral for Translation (DGT), Luxembourg)
Dr. Cristina EspañaBonet (Technical University of Catalonia, TALP, Barcelona)
Dr. Declan Groves (Center for Next Generation Localisation, Dublin City University, Ireland)
Prof. Jan Hajic (Institute of Formal and Applied Linguistics, Charles University in Prague)
Prof. Timo Honkela (Aalto University, Finland)
Dr. Patrick Lambert (LIUM University of Le Mans, France)
Prof. Qun Liu (Institute of Computing Technology, Chinese Academy of Sciences, China)
Dr. Maite Melero (Barcelona Media Innovation Center, Spain)
Dr. Tsuyoshi Okita (Dublin City University, Ireland)
Prof. Pavel Pecina (Institute of Formal and Applied Linguistics, Charles University in Prague)
Dr. Marta R. Costajussà (Barcelona Media Innovation Center, Spain)
Dr. Felipe Sanchez Martinez (Escuela Politecnica Superior, Universidad de Alicante, Spain)
Dr. Nicolas Stroppa (Google, Zurich, Switzerland)
Prof. Hans Uszkoreit (German Research Center for Artificial Intelligence, Germany)
Dr. David Vilar (German Research Center for Artificial Intelligence, Germany)

Table of Contents

Second Workshop on Applying Machine Learning Techniques to Optimise the Division of Labour in Hybrid MT

Program

Saturday, 15 December 2012

09:00–09:15	Josef van Genabith — Welcome and introductory remarks
09:15–09:40	*Hybrid Adaptation of Named Entity Recognition for Statistical Machine Translation* Vassilina Nikoulina, Agnes Sandor and Marc Dymetman
09:40–10:05	*Confusion Network Based System Combination for Chinese Translation Output: Word-Level or Character-Level?* Maoxi Li and MingWen Wang
10:05–10:30	*Using Cross-Lingual Explicit Semantic Analysis for Improving Ontology Translation* Kartik Asooja, Jorge Gracia, Nitish Aggarwal and Asunción Gómez Pérez
10:30–10:50	*System Combination with Extra Alignment Information* Xiaofeng Wu, Tsuyoshi Okita, Josef van Genabith and Qun Liu
10:50–11:10	*Topic Modeling-based Domain Adaptation for System Combination* Tsuyoshi Okita, Antonio Toral and Josef van Genabith
11:10–11:30	*Sentence-Level Quality Estimation for MT System Combination* Tsuyoshi Okita, Raphaël Rubino and Josef van Genabith
11:30–11:45	Tea break
11:45–12:05	*Neural Probabilistic Language Model for System Combination* Tsuyoshi Okita
12:05–12:25	*System Combination Using Joint, Binarised Feature Vectors* Christian Federmann
12:25–12:30	*Results from the ML4HMT-12 Shared Task on Applying Machine Learning Techniques to Optimise the Division of Labour in Hybrid Machine Translation* Christian Federmann, Tsuyoshi Okita, Maite Melero, Marta R. Costa-Jussa, Toni Badia and Josef van Genabith
12:30–12:50	**Discussion Panel** Panelists: Marc Dymetman (TBC), Jan Hajič, Qun Liu (TBC), Hans Uszkoreit, Josef van Genabith Topics include: • The Future of Hybrid MT: is there a single-paradigm winner? • Will we see increasing usage of additional, potentially highly sparse, features? • Will research efforts in Machine Translation and Machine Learning converge? • How do we evaluate progress in terms of translation quality for Hybrid MT? • What are the baselines? Can Human Judgment be integrated?
12:50–13:30	**Invited talk:** *Deep Linguistic Information in Hybrid Machine Translation* Jan Hajič, Institute of Formal and Applied Linguistics, Charles University in Prague

Hybrid Adaptation of Named Entity Recognition for Statistical Machine Translation

Vassilina NIKOULINA Agnes SANDOR Marc DYMETMAN
Xerox Research Center Europe, 6, chemin de Maupertuis,Meylan,FRANCE
vassilina.nikoulina@xrce.xerox.com, agnes.sandor@xrce.xerox.com,
marc.dymetman@xrce.xerox.com

ABSTRACT
Appropriate Named Entity handling is important for Statistical Machine Translation. In this work we address the challenging issues of generalization and sparsity of NEs in the context of SMT. Our approach uses the source NE Recognition (NER) system to generalize the training data by replacing the recognized Named Entities with place-holders, thus allowing a Phrase-Based Statistical Machine Translation (PBMT) system to learn more general patterns. At translation time, the recognized Named Entities are handled through a specifically adapted translation model, which improves the quality of their translation. We add a post-processing step to a standard NER system in order to make it more suitable for integration with SMT and we also learn a prediction model for deciding between options for translating the Named Entities, based on their context and on their impact on the translation of the entire sentence. We show important improvements in terms of BLEU and TER scores already after integration of NER into SMT, but especially after applying the SMT-adapted post-processing step to the NER component.

KEYWORDS: Named Entity Recognition, Statistical Machine Translation.

1 Introduction

The correct handling of Named Entities is not an easy task for Statistical Machine Translation. First, Named Entities — person names, organization names, dates, etc. — create a lot of sparsity in the training data. Second, Named Entities of the same type tend to occur in the same context, and thus, they should be treated in a similar way, but a phrase-based SMT model has limited capacity to learn this purely out of data. Finally, Named Entities can be ambiguous (eg. Bush in George Bush vs. blackcurrent bush), and a wrong NE translation can seriously hurt the final quality of the translation.

We propose a framework for integrating Named Entities within SMT, which tries to address all these issues at the same time. First, we try to generalize occurrences of Named Entities in the training data, by replacing the identified named entities by a small number of typed placeholders (one for each NE type: DATE, ORGANIZATION, ...) in order to reduce the sparsity problem, but still preserving some context for the purpose of SMT (all the dates tend to occur in similar contexts, different from the contexts in which person names occur). This generalization allows us to learn a better translation model, and to re-use the generalized patterns for rare (or unseen) Named Entities, in order to ensure a better translation for these NEs. Second, an external NE-translator (or multiple NE-translators for different NE types) is integrated in this framework, thus ensuring correct NE translation.

Third, we address the problem of adapting the NER system itself specifically for the purpose of improving the SMT task. There are few works reporting significant improvements over a baseline after Named Entities integration[1] (eg. from 8.7 to 13.3 of BLEU for Bangla-English (Pal et al., 2010), from 47 to 48.7 of BLEU for Hindi-English (Huang, 2005)). Others report rather low (sometimes negative) impact of Named Entity integration with SMT (0.3 BLEU gain for French-English in (Bouamor et al., 2012), 0.2 BLEU gain for Arabic-English in (Hermjakob et al., 2008), 1 BLEU loss for Chinese-English in (Agrawal and Singla, 2010)).

This is a disappointing result given how important correct NE translation is for overall translation quality. Possible reasons for this result (some of them identified in (Hermjakob et al., 2008)) include:

- Errors of the Named Entity Recognizer itself;
- The external NE-translator is often blind to the type of the NE; however, different treatments can be necessary for different types (e.g. some entities may require transliteration, others a specific kind of translation, and still others should not be translated);
- Often the integration of Named Entities is done by constraining a phrase-based model to producing a single candidate translation for a NE (as generated by an external NE translator): this may prevent the phrase-based model from using known phrases containing the same NE in a larger context, which might have led to more accurate translations.

We note that standard NER systems are designed for Information Extraction tasks and that the Named Entity structure required for these tasks may be different from that required for SMT. In this work we study how the NE structure may be adapted for integration within SMT and

[1]Note that not all works explicitly report the gain due to NE integration, but rather the joint gains due to the multiple factors involved. We only mention works in which the specific impact of the NER component is reported explicitly.

propose a post-processing method for a standard NER system in order to adapt this structure. We also propose a way to restrict the use of an external NE translator to those cases where calling it is really useful for the SMT task. First, we apply a set of general rules in order to make the NE structure more suitable for SMT. Next, we develop a prediction model which is able to choose for each NE which translation model is the best to translate it: either an external NE-translator (possibly chosen between multiple options), or the standard SMT model (in this case no special treatment is done for this NE).

The remainder of this paper is organized as follows. Section 2 describes our approach: we first present the general framework we propose for NER integration within SMT, and we then describe the post-processing and prediction steps for NER, which make NE integration more suitable for SMT. Section 3 presents an overview of the related work. Section 4 describes the experimental results and we conclude in Section 5.

2 Proposed Approach for the NE-enriched SMT model

2.1 Translation architecture

The framework that we propose can be summarized by the steps illustrated in the following example:

Src: *This paper illustrates the actions scheduled in Measure 6.2 " Co-operation in agriculture " of the Programme of the European Initiative Interreg II Italy - Albania, being implemented in Apulia since 1996.*

(1) First, we detect Named Entities in the source sentence and replace them with place-holders defined by the type of the NE (eg. DATE, ORGANIZATION, LOCATION): this gives us two types of objects that we need to translate: *reduced source sentences* (source sentences with place-holders) and original *named entities*;

Reduced Src: *This paper illustrates the actions scheduled in Measure 6.2 " Co-operation in agriculture " of the Programme of the European Initiative Interreg II +NE_LOCORG_COUNTRY - +NE_LOCORG_COUNTRY , being implemented in +NE_LOCORG_CITY since +NE_DATE .*

NEs: *Italy[LOCORG_COUNTRY], Albania[LOCORG_COUNTRY], Apulia[LOCORG_CITY], 1996[DATE]*

(2.1) The *reduced translation model* (able to deal with the place-holders) is applied to the reduced source sentence and generates a reduced translation:

Reduced Translation: *cet article illustre les actions prévues dans la mesure 6.2 " la coopération en agriculture " du programme de l' initiative interreg II +NE_LOCORG_COUNTRY - +NE_LOCORG_COUNTRY , mis en oeuvre à +NE_LOCORG_CITY depuis +NE_DATE .*

(2.2) An external NE translator is used for translating the replaced NEs; In principle, multiple NE translators can be used, depending on the nature of the Named Entity: a NE can stay untranslated or be transliterated (eg. PERSON), or its translation can be based on hand-crafted or automatically learned rules (eg. UNITS, 20°C = 68°F), or on an external Named Entity dictionary (which can be extracted from Wikipedia or from the parallel texts):

NE translation: *Italy=Italie, Albania=Albanie, Apulia=Pouilles, 1996=1996*

(3) Finally, Named Entity translations are re-inserted into the reduced translation (this uses the alignment produced internally by the SMT system for deciding which target place-holder corresponds to each source place-holder).

Complete Translation: *cet article illustre les actions prévues dans la mesure 6.2 " la coopération en agriculture " du programme de l' initiative interreg II Italie - Albanie , mis en oeuvre à Pouilles depuis 1996 .*

This integration of NER into SMT already addresses several problems of NE translation:

- First, assuming that NER is able to detect named entities, the approach avoids wrongly translating a NE as if it were a standard lexical expression;
- Second, the approach can translate NEs differently based on their identified type;
- Third, the reduced translation model is based on a generalization of training data which reduces sparsity, and, as a consequence, is able to learn a better model: the generalized patterns are helpful for dealing with rare or unseen Named Entities (eg. the bi-phrase *on +NE_DATE = le +NE_DATE* can be used to translate any date, and not only those seen in the training data).

2.2 NER adaptation for SMT

A weak point of our architecture is that the identification and processing of NEs is only loosely dependent on the SMT task. To get a tighter integration, we apply a post-processing method to the output of the NER system in order 1) to modify the NE structure for a better fit with SMT, and 2) to choose the NEs that have a potential to improve the final translation. We propose a hybrid post-processing, where:

- first, on each source sentence, a set of post-processing rules is applied to the NER output,
- second, a prediction model is applied to the NER output in order to choose only those Named Entities for specific NE-translation that can actually be helpful for SMT purposes; the prediction model is trained to optimize the final translation evaluation score.

We show empirically the importance of each of these steps in section 4.

2.2.1 Rule-based adaptation of NER systems for SMT purposes

Since numerous high-quality NER systems are ready to use, it is more reasonable to take advantage of them for SMT than to develop a new NER system from scratch. NER systems are usually developed for the purposes of information extraction, where the NEs are inserted in a task-motivated template. This template determines the scope and form of NEs. In the case of SMT the "templates" into which the NEs are inserted are sentences. This means that the NEs should be defined according to sentence-translation oriented criteria, because this ensures better quality of the model acquired from sentences containing place-holders for the named entities. In other words, the place-holders should not introduce a similar sparsity factor into the translation model to what the original NEs did. Thus existing NER systems may need some adaptation for SMT.

We consider the following requirements for designing the scope and the form of the NEs for SMT:

- The NEs extracted should not contain common nouns that might be relevant in an IE system, but do not need special translation: titles (Mr, Vice-President, etc.) and various other common nouns (street, road, number etc.). These elements should be removed from the scope of the NEs for SMT, and should be translated as parts of the reduced sentence, and not in the NE translation system.
- The NEs are embedded in various syntactic structures in the sentences, and often the units labeled as named entities contain structural elements in order to yield semantically meaningful units for IE. These structural elements are useful for training the reduced SMT model, and thus they should not be part of the NE. E.g. *le 1er janvier* should rather produce *DATE(1er janvier)* than *DATE(le 1er janvier)*.

The adaptation is rule-based. Given an existing NER system, the adaptation is executed along the following steps:

1 Extract NEs from a corpus relevant to the domain;

2 Either manually or automatically identify the list of common nouns within the NEs (titles, geographical nouns, etc.);

3 Either manually or automatically identify the list of function words at the beginning of NEs;

4a If the NER system is a black box:

  - Define rules (e.g. POS tagging, list, pattern matching) to recognize the common nouns and the function words in the output of the NER system;
  - Post-process the NEs extracted so that the common nouns and the function words are deleted;

4b If the source code of the NER system is available: Modify the source code so that the common nouns and function words do not get extracted.

2.2.2 Machine Learning extension of NER adaptation

The previously defined rules allow us to deal with a segmentation of Named Entities that is more suitable for SMT purposes: e.g. this segmentation may separate clearly the non-translatable units composing a person name from its context (ex: Mr.[context] White[non-translatable unit]). However, the importance of certain NEs or NE types for SMT may vary across different domains and text styles. It may also be dependent on the SMT model itself: simple Named Entities that are frequent in the data on which SMT was trained are already well-translated by a baseline model, while the call for an external NE-translator will make the process more complex, and in some cases, produce worse results (due to the lack of context).

The impact of one specific Named Entity on the final translation quality may depend on different factors: NE context, NE frequency in the training data, the type of the NE, the reliability of NE-translator, etc. The impact of each of these factors may be heterogeneous across different domains and styles of the text, and a rule-based approach is not suitable to address this problem in its generality.

We propose to learn a *prediction model*, based on the features that control these different aspects, which will be able to predict the impact that the special treatment of a specific Named Entity could potentially have on the final translation. The main objective of this model is to select only NEs that can improve the final translation, and reject the NEs that can hurt or make no difference for the final translation. In order to achieve this objective, we create an appropriate training set as described below.

In what follows we refer to the baseline SMT model as SMT and to the NE-enriched SMT model as SMT_{NE}. For the prediction training we create a labelled training set out of a set of parallel sentences $(s_i, t_i), i = 1..N$.

- For each $i = 1..N$:
  - translate s_i with the baseline SMT model: $SMT(s_i)$;
  - For each NE ne_k found by NER (and post-processed by a rule-based step) in s_i:
    - translate $s_i|_{ne_k}$ with the NER enriched SMT model: $SMT_{NE}(s_i|_{ne_k})$; ne_k is replaced by a place-holder in s_i, and external NE-translator is used to translate ne_k;
    - compare $SMT(s_i)$ and $SMT_{NE}(s_i|_{ne_k})$ by comparing them to the reference translation t_i: we denote the corresponding evaluation scores by $score(SMT_{NE}(s_i|_{ne_k}))$, $score(SMT(s_i))$ (we may use any standard MT evaluation metric, suitable for sentence-level evaluation);
    - the label of the named entity ne_k is based on the comparison between $score(SMT_{NE}(s_i|_{ne_k}))$ and $score(SMT(s_i))$: positive if $score(SMT_{NE}(s_i|_{ne_k})) > score(SMT(s_i))$ (meaning that NE-enriched system produces a better translation than a baseline), and negative otherwise.

A classification model trained on a training set created in this way will be optimized (by construction) to choose the NEs that improve the final translation quality; the features for this classification model are detailed in section 4.2.2.

This method can also be extended for the case where multiple NE translation systems are available: eg. do not translate/transliterate (person names), rule-based (eg. UNITS, 20°C =

68°F), dictionary based, etc. In this case the translation prediction model can be transformed into a multi-class labelling problem, where each class corresponds to the model that should be chosen for a particular NE translation model (including the model that do nothing and let baseline the SMT model to deal with NE translation).

2.3 Training NE-enriched SMT

To apply he translation framework described above, first, we need to train a reduced translation model that is capable of dealing with the place-holders correctly. The training of the reduced translation model requires a reduced parallel corpus (a corpus with both source and target Named Entities replaced with place-holders). In order to keep consistency between source and target Named Entities we project the source Named Entities to the target part of the corpus using the statistical word-alignment model (obtained with GIZA++, similar to (Huang and Vogel, 2002)).

Next, we train a phrase-based statistical translation model on the corpus obtained in this way, which allows us to learn generalized patterns (eg. *on +NE_DATE = le +NE_DATE)* for better NE treatment. The replaced Named Entity and its projection are stored separately in a Named Entity dictionary that can then be re-used for NE translation.

When every source Named Entity that was correctly projected to the target sentence is systematically replaced by a place-holder, the translation model trained on such a corpus will not be able to translate the original NEs (they will never or very rarely occur in the resulting training data). This is in contradiction with our prediction model, which may choose to replace or not a NE with a place-holder depending on its context, requiring the ability to translate both a reduced and a non-reduced sentence.

In order to meet this requirement we train a hybrid NE-enriched model, which replaces a NE by a place-holder with probability α: a model trained on a corpus created in this way will indeed be able to translate the frequent NEs in their original form, but at the same time it allows generalization (which is especially important for rare NEs). This hybrid model was inspired by (Bisazza and Federico, 2012), where a hybrid LM was trained in a similar way.[2]

Possible models for the NE-translator include:

- NEs extracted out of parallel corpora by projection of source NEs on the target side can be re-used as NE-translations at the translation step;
- another option is to create an adapted SMT model for NE translation: perform tuning of the baseline PBMT on the subset of extracted NEs (such a model can be useful for the Named Entities that should be translated, but are not directly available in the NE dictionary, eg. *General Division of Land Management, Housing and Patrimony* [ORGANIZATION])

3 Related Work

The mainstream approach for Named Entity integration into an SMT framework is to detect a NE (with an existing NER) and apply an external translation model (NE-translator) to translate the detected NE. The translation proposed by the external model is then integrated into SMT

[2]In our experiments, we take $\alpha = 0.5$.

a) as a default translation (Li et al., 2009; Huang and Vogel, 2002), b) added dynamically to the phrase-based table to compete with other phrases (Turchi et al., 2012; Hermjakob et al., 2008; Bouamor et al., 2012), c) replaced by a fake (non-translatable) value, which is replaced by the initial Named Entity once the translation is done (applied for non-translatable NE in (Tinsley et al., 2012)).

This approach mainly addresses the disambiguation issue when translating Named Entities (given that NER is actually able to disambiguate properly), in order to guarantee a correct NE translation.

The sparsity problem is partially addressed either by extracting bilingual Named Entities from the parallel corpus and appending them to the training data, in order to improve the alignment procedure (Bouamor et al., 2012; Okita et al., 2010). However, this approach does not allow to generalize the information learned from the training data for new, unseen Named Entities.

Several "soft" integrations of the NE-translator were previously suggested (Turchi et al., 2012; Hermjakob et al., 2008; Bouamor et al., 2012), where a translation proposed by the NE-translator competes with other phrases of the phrase-table. This allows not to decrease the final translation quality when a wrong NE is proposed by the NER system (either because it is not suitable for an external NE-translator, or because of an error has been done by NER). But this approach does not allow to correct the output of the NER system, and at best it allows simply not to decrease the translation quality due to a wrongly-formed Named Entity, but there is no possibility to improve the final translation in this approach.

The closest work to ours is the one by (Hermjakob et al., 2008), who addresses a problem of NE transliteration for Arabic-English translation. Similar to our approach, the authors propose to adapt the transliteration model for the translation task, and to "learn" when the transliteration is actually helpful for SMT, rather than trust blindly the NER and transliterate every output of the NER system (which may often introduce new errors). However, the way this adaptation is done is very different from what we propose. It relies on annotations done on the parallel training corpus, where each Arabic token/phrase is marked if its transliteration is found in the corresponding English sentence. This annotated corpus is then used to train a transliteration model. However it is not straightforward that the thus learned transliteration model is actually one that improves the final translation quality: the authors report similar results in terms of BLEU to those of a baseline SMT, although the model appears to improve the Named Entities translation (measured in terms of NEWA (Hermjakob et al., 2008)). This indicates that although overall NE translations were improved, probably the context in which they occurred was less accurate, or in some cases the errors done by NER (or the transliterator) led to worse translation. Our NER postprocessing approach optimizes explicitly the final translation score, and can actually be complementary to the approach taken by (Hermjakob et al., 2008). Moreover, some heuristics used by (Hermjakob et al., 2008) (such as applying the transliteration model only to NEs that occurred less than 50 times in training data) can be taken into account in our approach in a more flexible way, at the same time as other important features (e.g. the context in which NE occurs, the confidence of the proposed transliteration etc.).

Table 1: Statistics for the train and test data.

Data set	Nb units	Nb tokens En	Nb tokens Fr
train	152525	3176875	2914542
extra monolingual data	118946	-	4331604
dev-set, MERT-tuning	1100	36484	40474
dev-set, NE prediction mode	1100	36672	41052
test-abstracts	426	45115	58549
test-titles	2000	23888	30786

4 Experiments

4.1 Data and baseline

The training set of parallel sentences was further extended with a subset of the JRC-Aquis[3] corpus, based on the domain-related Eurovoc categories. Overall, the in-domain training data consist of 3M tokens per language.

We have extracted two development sets containing both abstracts and titles. The first dev-set was used for the MERT optimisation of the NE-reduced translation model. The second dev-set was used for training the NE prediction model2.2.2. Both dev-sets were extracted from truly in-domain data (INRA & FAO)

We tested our approach on two different types of texts extracted from in-domain data: 2000 titles (test-titles) and 500 abstracts (test-abstracts). Statistics about the train and test data are given in table 1.

We used a phrase-based SMT model trained by Moses(Koehn et al., 2007) with standard Moses settings (5-gramm LM, lexicalized reordering) on this data as the baseline translation system for our experiments.

4.2 NER adaptation

4.2.1 Rule-based NER adaptation

As a baseline NER system we used the NER component of the Xerox Incremental Parser (XIP (Aït-Mokhtar et al., 2002)) for English. The baseline NER system is rule-based and recognizes a large number of different Named Entities: date, person, numerical expressions, location names, organization names, events.

We ran XIP on a development corpus and extracted lists of NEs: PERSON, ORGANISATION, LOCATION, DATE. We then identified a list of common names and function words that should be eliminated from the NEs. In the XIP grammar NEs are extracted by local grammar rules as groups of labels that are the POS categories of the terminal lexical nodes in the parse tree. The post-processing consisted in re-writing the original groups of labels by ones that exclude the unnecessary common nouns and function words (see section 2.2.1).

[3]http://langtech.jrc.it/JRC-Acquis.html

4.2.2 Prediction model for choosing NE translation model

The prediction model for SMT adaptation relies on the following features:

- Named Entity frequency in the training data;
- confidence in the translation of NE dictionary; (if ne_s: source named entity, ne_t: translation suggested for ne_s by NE dictionary, we measure confidence as $p(ne_t|ne_s)$ estimated on the training data used to create NE dictionary);
- a collection of features defined by the context of the Named Entity: the number of features in this collection corresponds to the number of trigrams that occur in the training data of the following type: a named entity place-holder extended with its 1-word left and right context (eg. *the +NE_DATE,*);
- the probability of the Named Entity in the context, estimated from the source corpus (3-gram Language Model);
- the probability of the place-holder replacing a Named Entity in the context (3-gram reduced Language Model);

The corpus used to train the prediction model contains 2000 sentences (a mixture of titles and abstracts). A labelled training set is created out of a parallel set as described in 2.2.2. We used the TER (translation edit rate) score for measuring individual sentence scores. Overall, we obtain 461 labelled samples, with 172 positive examples, 183 negative examples, and 106 neutral examples (the samples where both SMT_{NE} and SMT provide the same translation). We learn a 3-class SVM prediction model and we choose to replace only the NEs that are classified as positive at test time.

4.3 NE-enriched SMT training

We train a hybrid reduced translation model replacing a Named Entity by a place-holder with probability $\alpha = 0.5$ as described in section 2.3. The NE-translator performs as follows:

- First, it checks whether a NE translation is available in the NE dictionary extracted from the parallel corpus (which contains 11347 entries);
- If no translation is found in the NE dictionary, a baseline SMT model, with weights tuned on a subset of NEs extracted from the parallel corpus, is used as a back-off.

4.4 Evaluation

We evaluate the performance of different translation models using both BLEU (Papineni et al., 2001) and TER (Snover et al., 2006) metrics. We compare the following translation models:

- SMT: a baseline phrase-based statistical translation model without Named Entity treatment;
- $SMT_{NE-baseline}$: NE-enriched SMT (described in 2.1) where the baseline NER is used (no NER post-processing is done);

- RB-adapted SMT_{NE-RB} : SMT_{NE} where only the first post-processing step (rule-based NE structure modification described in 2.2.1) is applied to the baseline NER;
- SMT_{NE-ML}: SMT_{NE} where only the second post-processing step (prediction model described in 2.2.2) is applied to the baseline NER;
- $SMT_{NE-full}$: SMT_{NE} relying both on rule-based and machine learning post-processing steps for NER.

We also compare the results of our NE-enriched system to the approach used by (Turchi et al., 2012) where the NE translations provided by an external dictionary (the NE dictionary extracted from the parallel corpus in our case) are suggested as dynamic bi-phrases (using Moses XML tagging mechanism) to the decoder. We refer to the approach used in (Turchi et al., 2012) as $SMT_{NE-Turchi}$; this is the soft NE integration into the model (soft XML tagging option of Moses), which may choose the NE translation between the one suggested by the NE dictionary and the one suggested by the baseline SMT during the decoding process. In principle, this NE integration is more flexible than the pipeline approach we adopt. However, this approach does not have the generalization capability of our NE-enriched model.

Table 2: Results for NER adaptation for SMT

Model	**test-titles**		**test-abstracts**	
	BLEU	TER	BLEU	TER
SMT (baseline)	0.3135	0.6566	0.1148	0.8935
$SMT_{NE-Turchi}$	0.3135	0.6565	0.1149	0.8934
$SMT_{NE-baseline}$	0.3213	0.6636	0.1211	0.9064
SMT_{NE-RB}	0.3258	0.6605	0.1257	0.8968
SMT_{NE-ML}	0.3371	0.6523	0.1228	0.9050
$SMT_{NE-full}$	**0.3421**	**0.6443**	**0.1341**	**0.8935**

The translation results for the models described above are reported in Table 2.

First, we abstract from NER adaptation, and compare two approaches relying on the non-adapted NER, to evaluate our NE-enriched SMT model. We show that our approach $SMT_{NE-baseline}$ performs better than $SMT_{NE-Turchi}$. We believe that this gain is due to the generalization capacity of our model. Indeed, since the training data we used is relatively small, the sparsity issue is very important in this setting, and the capacity to generalize the observed NE occurrences helps our model. We see that $SMT_{NE-Turchi}$ performance is very close to the baseline SMT. This is probably due to the fact that the only NEs that are integrated are those that are already present in the training corpus, and no external knowledge was injected. This is, however, also the case for our model, and we believe that adding an external NE dictionary might improve both models.

Second, we note that each of the NER adaptation post-processing steps (SMT_{NE-RB} and SMT_{NE-ML}) brings improvements compared to the case when non-adapted NER is used ($SMT_{NE-baseline}$). Finally, we see that the combination of both steps gives the best results, which proves that these two steps complement each other and are both important for the final translation quality.

Table 3: Named Entity density in the test data

NE type	test-titles		test-abstracts	
	NEs detected	NEs selected	NEs detected	NEs selected
DATE	191	48 (25%)	121	32 (26%)
LOCATION	127	28 (22%)	61	20 (32%)
LOCORG	614	190 (30%)	189	44 (23%)
ORGANISATION	132	38 (28%)	210	33 (15%)
PERSON	95	44 (46%)	79	31 (39%)
EVENT	3	1 (33%)	3	0
UNIT	6	0	82	3 (3%)
PERCENT	2	1 (50%)	84	20 (23%)
Total	1170	350 (29%)	823	183 (22%)

4.4.1 Error analysis

We have performed some error analysis to find out the interaction between various aspects of our model with the final translation performance.

First, we carried out a small-scale manual evaluation of NER over around 500 entities for English. The recall of for all the NEs (including non-detectable NE types) was 53% and the precision was 86%. The types of NEs not detected but potentially relevant were projects, titles and biological entities. The worse performance among detectable NE types was observed for the organization names (precision: 80%, recall: 68%). This performance can be explained by the domain specificity of our data which is very different from the one (news articles) which was used for NER development.

Second, we looked at the NE density in the corpus and how the integration of the prediction model impacts it. Table 3 reports the number of different NEs (by type) detected in total in each test set, and the number of NEs that were selected by the prediction model (meaning that the integration of these NEs has the potential to improve the final translation). First, we see that we select only 29% of the total entities detected in the titles test set, and even fewer (22%) in the abstracts test set. We also observe that NEs density is lower in the abstracts than in the titles, and that the frequency of NE types differs between titles and abstracts: abstracts contain more UNIT and PERCENT types, which are less ambiguous and easier to handle for the baseline SMT. The above mentioned points may also explain lower impact after NE integration on the abstracts test.

We see that the NEs most frequently retained by the prediction model are the PERSON names which are probably the most sparse entities, which can be translated independently of the context. We also see that we retain much fewer ORGANISATION types in the abstracts test compared to the titles test: this is due to the fact that the organization names that occur in the titles are frequent acronyms (eg. FAO, ONU, INRA) which are well handled by NER, while abstracts contain more ambigous and difficult to detect organization names (eg. table 4, ex.3: Confederation of Agricultural Workers).

Finally, table 4 shows some examples extracted from each of the tests on how NE integration impacts the final translation. We see some cases where it is important to have a separate

Table 4: Examples of English-French translations with and without NE integration.

	test-titles
1	**Src:** Comparison of the **morphometric indexes** of the grasshopper tippet Schistocerca **gregaria Forskael**, 1775 at **Adrar** and at Tamanrasset (Sahara, Algeria) in 1995 **Baseline:** Comparaison **de l'étude de l'index** grasshopper tippet Schistocerca **gregaria, Forskael** 1775 sur **tomate** et à Tamanrasset (Sahara algérien) en 1995 **NE-full:** Comparaison **des indices morphometriques** de la grasshopper tippet Schistocerca **gregaria Forskael**, 1775 sur le terrain à **Adrar** et à Tamanrasset (Sahara algérien) en 1995
2	**Src:** Decisions in favour of the future generations. Proceedings of the Conference, Brussels, **8 May 1996** [with contributions of George, S.; Rahman A.; Alders, H.; Platteau, J.P.] **Baseline:** Les décisions en faveur des générations futures. Compte rendu de la conférence, bruxelles, **8 peut 1996** [avec les apports de George, S.; Rahman A.; l'aulne, H.; Platteau, J.P.] **NE-full:** Les décisions en faveur des générations futures. Compte rendu de la conférence, bruxelles, **le 8 mai 1996** [avec les apports de George, S.; Rahman A.; l'aulne, H.; Platteau, J.P.]
	test-abstracts
3	**Src:** The Author , **F. Mellozzini** , carries out an in - depth analysis of the objectives of agricultural policy which have arisen during a meeting on " Which kind of agriculture for the 1980 's? " held in Rome by the **Confederation of Agricultural Workers on 18 - 19 October** . **Baseline:** L'auteur, **F., Mellozzini** exerce une analyse des objectifs de la politique agricole qui ont ainsi présentée au cours de la réunion, sur " dont la nature de l'agriculture de la 1980 ? " tenue à Rome par la **mobilité des salariés agricoles sur 18 - 19 octobre**. **NE-full:** L'auteur, **F. Mellozzini**, exerce une analyse approfondie des objectifs de la politique agricole qui ont ainsi présentée au cours de la réunion sur " qui la nature de l'agriculture pour 1980 ? " tenue à Rome par la **confédération des travailleurs agricoles en 18 - 19 octobre**.
5	**Src:** These studies allowed the drawing up of a balance of its qualities and limits observed , its effectiveness in natural conditions and provide the opportunity to share some ideas on the use **in Africa of the South American auxiliary** . **Baseline:** ces études ont permis l'établissement d'un bilan de ses qualités et limites observés, son efficacité en conditions naturelles et prévoir la possibilité d'action des idées sur l'utilisation **en Afrique du Sud auxiliaires américaine.** **NE-full:**Ces études ont permis l'établissement d'un bilan de ses qualités et limites observés, son efficacité en conditions naturelles et de prévoir la possibilité à part quelques idées sur l'utilisation en **Afrique des auxiliaires d'Amérique du Sud.**
3	**Src:** Farmers are willing to pay between **13.5 percent and 14.5 percent** of the value of the premium rate demanded by insurance companies . **Baseline:** les agriculteurs sont prêts à payer **pour cent entre 13.5 et 14.5 pour cent** de la valeur de la prime taux exigées par les sociétés d'assurance. **NE-full:** les agriculteurs sont prêts à payer **entre 13,5 pour cent et 14,5 pour cent** de la valeur de la prime taux demandées par les compagnies d'assurance.

translation model for the NE itself (ex. 1, 2, 3 and 5). At the same time, we see that although the NE translation did not change, the surrounding context was better translated: ex. 3 "*sur DATE*" vs "*en DATE*", ex.4 : *auxiliary* was better placed in the translation.

Finally, we would like to note that our test set is rather difficult both for NER, and for MT translation. We believe that application of the same NER integration on an easier data set (with higher NER performance) may lead to higher improvements.

5 Discussion and Perspectives

In this work we have addressed the main problems of Named Entities integration into an SMT framework. We have proposed an approach that is able to generalize the Named Entity context observed in the training data and re-use it for new (unseen) NE translations. Our approach can also integrate one or several external NE-translators, and allows to choose an adapted NE-translator for each NE. The choice of the adapted NE-translator model is done via a prediction model that relies on features specific to the NE itself, the context in which it occurs and also the baseline SMT model which is enriched with NER. In addition, we propose a set of NER post-processing rules that allow to modify the NE structure in order to produce better NE segmentation for integration within SMT. We have shown empirically that each aspect of our model is important, and that the combination of all of them leads to the best results (2-3 BLEU points improvement over a baseline for two different test sets).

This framework opens several possible future research directions. First, NER-SMT integration pipeline can be replaced by a confusion network representation, where the best NE translation model will be chosen internally by the decoder. The prediction model scores can serve a basis for assigning a score for each alternative path in the confusion network.

Second, the procedure of creating an annotated training set for learning the prediction model which optimizes the MT evaluation score (described at 2.2.2) can be applied to other tasks than NER adaptation. More generally it can be applied to any pre-processing step done before translation (eg. spell-checking, sentence simplification, reordering, or any other source modification which might help to produce a better translation). The advantage of applying a prediction model to these steps is to make the pre-processing model more flexible and better adapted to the SMT task it is applied to.

Finally, in our experiments we have only used three options for the NE-translator: a NE dictionary extracted out of parallel data, a SMT model tuned for NE translation and a baseline SMT model. There are many other options that need to be explored, among them integrating an external NE dictionary mined from Wikipedia or LinkedData or creating specific translation models for each NE type.

Acknowledgements

This work was partially supported by the Organic.Lingua project (http://www.organic-lingua.eu/), funded by the European Commission under the ICT Policy Support Programme (ICT PSP).

References

Agrawal, N. and Singla, A. (2010). Using named entity recognition to improve machine translation. Technical report, Standford University, Natural Language Processing.

Aït-Mokhtar, S., Chanod, J.-P., and Roux, C. (2002). Robustness beyond shallowness: incremental deep parsing. *Natural Language Engineering*, 8(3):121–144.

Bisazza, A. and Federico, M. (2012). Cutting the long tail: Hybrid language models for translation style adaptation. In *EACL 2012, 13th Conference of the European Chapter of the Association for Computational Linguistics, Avignon, France, April 23-27, 2012*, pages 439–448.

Bouamor, D., Semmar, N., and Zweigenbaum, P. (2012). Identifying multi-word expressions in statistical machine translation. In *In LREC 2012, Seventh International Conference on Language Resources and Evaluation*.

Hermjakob, U., Knight, K., and Daumé III, H. (2008). Name translation in statistical machine translation learning when to transliterate. In *Proceedings of ACL-08:HLT*.

Huang, F. (2005). *Multilingual Named Entity extraction and translation from text and speech*. PhD thesis, Language Technology Institute, School of Computer Science, Carnegie Mellon University.

Huang, F. and Vogel, S. (2002). Improved named entity translation and bilingual named entity extraction. In *Proceedings of the 4th IEEE International Conference on Multimodal Interfaces*, ICMI '02, pages 253–, Washington, DC, USA. IEEE Computer Society.

Koehn, P., Hoang, H., Birch, A., Callison-Burch, C., Federico, M., Bertoldi, N., Cowan, B., Shen, W., Moran, C., Zens, R., Dyer, C., Bojar, O., Constantin, A., and Herbst, E. (2007). Moses: open source toolkit for statistical machine translation. In *ACL '07: Proceedings of the 45th Annual Meeting of the ACL on Interactive Poster and Demonstration Sessions*, pages 177–180. Association for Computational Linguistics.

Li, M., Zhang, J., Zhou, Y., and Chengqing, Z. (2009). The CASIA statistical machine translation system for iwslt 2009. In *Proceedings of IWSLT 2009*.

Okita, T., Maldonado Guerra, A., Graham, Y., and Way, A. (2010). Multi-word expression-sensitive word alignment. In *Proceedings of the 4th Workshop on Cross Lingual Information Access*, pages 26–34, Beijing, China. Coling 2010 Organizing Committee.

Pal, S., Kimar Naskar, S., Pecina, P., Bandyopadhyay, S., and Way, A. (2010). Handling named entities and compound verbs in phrase-based statistical machine translation. In *Proceedings of the Workshop on Multiword Expressions: from Theory to Applications (MWE 2010)*.

Papineni, K., Roukos, S., Ward, T., and Zhu, W. (2001). Bleu: a method for automatic evaluation of machine translation.

Snover, M., Dorr, B., Schwartz, R., Micciulla, L., and Makhoul, J. (2006). A study of translation edit rate with targeted human annotation. In *In Proceedings of Association for Machine Translation in the Americas*, pages 223–231.

Tinsley, J., Ceausu, A., and Zhang, J. (2012). PLUTO: automated solutions for patent translation. In *EACL Joint Workshop on Exploitng Synergies between Information Retrieval and Machine Translation (ESIRMT) and Hybrid Approaches to Machine Translation (HyTra): Proceedings of the workshop, EACL 2012*.

Turchi, M., Atkinson, M., Wilcox, A., Crawley, B., Bucci, S., Steinberger, R., and Van der Goot, E. (2012). ONTS: "Optima" news translation system. In *Proceedings of the Demonstrations at the 13th Conference of the European Chapter of the Association for Computational Linguistics*.

Confusion Network Based System Combination for Chinese Translation Output: Word-Level or Character-Level?

LI Maoxi[1] *WANG Mingwen*[1]
(1) School of Computer Information Engineering, Jiangxi Normal University, Nanchang, China, 330022
moses1i@yeah.net, mwwang@jxnu.edu.cn

ABSTRACT

Recently, confusion network based system combination has applied successfully to various machine translation tasks. However, to construct the confusion network when combining the Chinese translation outputs from multiple machine translation systems, it is possible to either take a Chinese word as the atomic unit (word-level) or take a Chinese character as the atomic unit (character-level). In this paper, we compare word-level approach with character-level approach for combining Chinese translation outputs on the NIST'08 EC tasks and IWSLT'08 EC CRR challenge tasks. Our experimental results reveal that character-level combination system significantly outperforms word-level combination system.

KEYWORDS : machine translation; system combination; confusion network; Chinese translation output

1 Introduction

In recent years, the confusion network based system combination seems to be an expedient powerful means to improve the translation quality in many machine translation tasks empirically, which aims at combining the multiple outputs of various translation systems into a consensus translation (Chen et al., 2009; Feng et al., 2009; He et al., 2008; Rosti et al., 2007; Watanabe & Sumita, 2011). Confusion network based system combination picks one hypothesis as the skeleton and aligns the other hypotheses against the skeleton to form a confusion network. The path with the highest score represents the consensus translation.

Previous work on system combination most focus on combining translation outputs in Latin alphabet-based languages, in which sentences are already segmented into words sequences with white space before constructing the confusion network. However, for Asian Language, such as Chinese, Japanese, and Korean etc., words are not demarcated originally in the translation output. Thus, in those languages processing, the first step is to segment the translation output into a sequence of words. Instead of segmenting the translation output into words, an alternative is to split the translation output into characters, which can be readily done with perfect accuracy. It is possible that take either a word or a character as the smallest unit to construct the confusion network for system combination. So far, there has been no detailed study to compare the translation performance of these two combination approaches (word-level vs. character-level).

In this paper, we compare the translation performance of confusion network based system combination when the Chinese translation output is segmented into words versus characters. Since there are several Chinese word segmentation (CWS) tools that can segment Chinese sentences into words and their segmentation results are different, we use three representative CWS tools in our experiments. Our experimental results on the NIST'08 EC tasks and IWSLT'08 EC CRR challenge tasks reveal that character-level combination approach significantly outperforms word-level combination approach. That is, the Chinese translation outputs to be combined are not needed to be segment into words.

2 Related work

It is a long debating issue that which one, word or character, is the appropriate unit for Chinese natural language processing. J. Xu, et al. investigated CWS for Chinese-English phrase-based statistical machine translation (SMT), and found that a system which relied on characters performed slightly worse than when it used segmented words (Xu et al., 2004). R. Zhang, et al. reported that the most accurate word segmentation is not the best word segmentation for SMT (Zhang et al., 2008). P-C Chang, et al. optimized CWS granularity with respect to the SMT task (Chang et al., 2008). M. Li, et al. compared word-level metrics with character-level metrics, and demonstrated that word segmentation is not essential for automatic evaluation of Chinese translation output (Li et al., 2011). J. Du utilized a character-level system combination strategy to improve translation quality for English-Chinese spoken language translation (Du, 2011).

3 Confusion network based system combination for Chinese translation output

One of the crucial steps in confusion network based system combination is to align different hypotheses to each other. A variety of monolingual hypothesis alignment strategies have been proposed in recent years, such as GIZA++-like approach (Matusov et al., 2006; Och & Ney, 2003), TER (Snover et al., 2006), IHMM (He et al., 2008), and IncIHMM (Li et al., 2009) etc. It had been reported that IHMM is the most stable among the first three approaches (Chen et al., 2009). To get higher quality hypothesis alignment, we utilize the IHMM approach to align translation output.

IHMM approach uses a similarity model and a distortion model to calculate the conditional probability that the hypothesis is generated by the skeleton. The similarity model, which models the similarity between a word in the skeleton and a word in the hypothesis, is a linear interpolation of the semantic similarity and surface similarity.

$$p(e_j^{'} \mid e_i) = a \cdot p_{sem}(e_j^{'} \mid e_i) + (1-a) \cdot p_{sur}(e_j^{'} \mid e_i) \quad (1)$$

The interpolation weight α is empirically set as 0.3.

For Chinese translation output, the semantic similarity between two Chinese words or two Chinese characters can also be estimated by using the source word sequence as a hidden layer. Because it is very hard to get the longest matched prefix or the longest common subsequence between two Chinese words or two Chinese characters, the surface similarity is based on exact match, that is, the surface similarity is set 1 if the word or character e' is the same as e, and is set 0 otherwise.

Given a source sentence: "*Pakistan cleric says would rather die than surrender*" and three translation hypotheses: "*巴基斯坦称死不投诚*", "*巴基斯坦说死不投诚*", "*巴基斯坦说死于投诚*", we can use IHMM approach to align the hypotheses at character-level and word-level. The character-level and word-level confusion networks are built as shown in FIGURE 1. Finally, the consensus translation can be obtained by confusion network decoding.

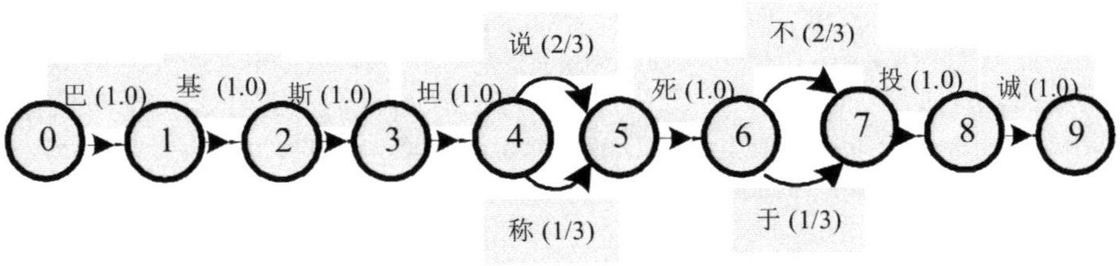

(a) A character-level confusion network

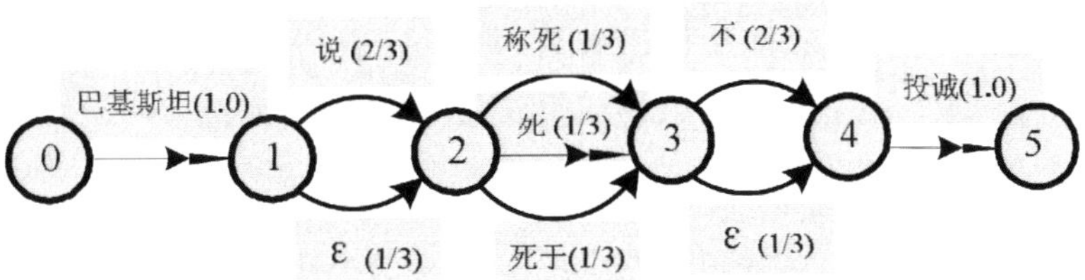

(b) A word-level confusion network

FIGURE 1-Character-level and word-level confusion networks

4 Experimental results

4.1 Data

To compare the performance of word-level combination system with character-level combination system, we conduct experiments on two datasets, in the newswire translation domain and the spoken language translation domain.

The test set of NIST'08 English-to-Chinese translation task contains 127 documents with 1,830 segments. Each segment has 4 reference translations and the system translations of 11 machine translation systems, released in the corpus LDC2010T01. The best 7 submitted system outputs from the constrained training track are chose to participate in system combination, and a 4-gram language model is trained on the official released data LDC2005T14. A 3-fold cross-validation is used to compare the combination performance, the test set is randomly partitioned into three parts, two of them are utilized as development set and the rest is utilized as test set.

Experiments on spoken language translation domain are carried out on the IWSLT'08 English-to-Chinese CRR challenge task. We use the bilingual training data provided by IWSLT evaluation campaign (Paul, 2008). The development set contained 757 segments and the test set contained 300 segments, each segment with 7 human reference translations.

4.2 Automatic evaluation of Chinese translation output

It has been reported that character-level automatic metrics correlate with human judgment better than word-level automatic metrics for Chinese translation evaluation (Li et al., 2011). To measure the translation performance of word-level combination system and character-level combination system, several off-the-shelf automatic metrics, namely BLEU (Papineni et al., 2002), NIST (Doddington, 2002), METEOR (Banerjee & Lavie, 2005), GTM (Melamed et al., 2003), and TER (Snover et al., 2006), are used at character-level. Unless otherwise stated, the performance of Chinese translation is measured with character-level metrics scores. Because better automatic evaluation metrics leading to better translation performance for parameters optimization (Liu et al., 2011), the feature weights of confusion network based combination system are tuned based on character-level BLEU score.

4.3 Results

For NIST'08 EC task, the submitted outputs of 7 systems are combined: system 01, system 03, system 17, system 18, system 24, system 28, and system 31. Due to words are not demarcated in the system outputs, we must divide the output into words or characters to facilitate hypothesis alignment before combining the outputs. Since there are a number of CWS tools and they generally give different segmentation results. To consistently segment the Chinese outputs into word sequences, we experimented with three different CWS tools, namely ICTCLAS (Zhang et al., 2003), Stanford Chinese word segmenter (STANFORD) (Tseng et al., 2005), Urheen (Wang et al., 2010). TABLE 1 summary the performance for character-level combination system and word-level combination systems. The "Character" row shows the translation performance after the system outputs are split into characters. The "ICTCLAS", "STANFORD", and "Urheen" rows show the scores when the system outputs are segmented into words by the respective CWS tools. Compared to word-level combination systems, the character-level combination system improves the translation performance. This improvement is statistically significant ($p < 0.01$).

TABLE 1-The performance of word-level systems and character-level system on NIST'08 EC task

Average	DEV					TST				
	BLEU	NIST	METEOR	GTM	TER	BLEU	NIST	METEOR	GTM	TER
system 01	33.38	8.67	48.51	73.91	56.56	33.38	8.45	48.51	73.96	56.56
system 03	38.06	8.52	50.35	73.94	51.73	38.06	8.26	50.35	73.96	51.73
system 17	31.30	7.47	44.99	68.10	56.45	31.30	7.26	44.99	68.15	56.45
system 18	32.02	7.23	45.24	68.46	56.51	32.02	7.03	45.24	68.52	56.51
system 24	40.04	9.35	52.14	**77.43**	**51.16**	40.04	9.07	52.14	**77.48**	**51.16**
system 28	33.60	7.86	46.71	70.85	57.58	33.60	7.64	46.71	70.91	57.58
system 31	**40.04**	**9.62**	**52.94**	77.29	51.99	**40.04**	**9.33**	**52.94**	77.37	51.99
ICTCLAS	40.63	9.48	52.03	78.41	52.96	40.44	9.18	51.86	78.14	53.11
STANFORD	40.27	9.44	51.69	78.59	53.89	40.05	9.13	51.60	78.48	54.00
Urheen	40.13	9.39	51.60	78.17	53.44	39.91	9.06	51.47	77.91	53.51
Character	**42.73**	**9.90**	**53.99**	**79.63**	**51.15**	**42.71**	**9.58**	**53.97**	**79.52**	**51.08**

Besides combining the submitted system outputs in which words are not delimited on NIST'08 EC task, we also conduct experiments on system outputs that have been segmented into word sequences on IWSLT'08 EC CRR challenge tasks. The state of the art SMT systems, Moses (Koehn et al., 2006) and Joshua (Li et al., 2009), are exploited to generate N-best lists for system combination. We segment the Chinese sentences in bilingual training data into word sequences, and train several English-to-Chinese SMT systems to decode the development set and test set of IWSLT'08 EC CRR challenge tasks. The N-best list hypotheses can be seemed to have been segmented into words by the same CWS tool that is used to segment the Chinese sentences in the training data.

TABLE 2 shows the translation performance when translation outputs to be combined are with different word granularity. Two SMT systems are combined: $\text{Joshua}_{\text{ICTCLAS}}$, and $\text{Joshua}_{\text{STANFORD}}$. $\text{Joshua}_{\text{ICTCLAS}}$ represent the Joshua system that Chinese sentences in the training data have been segmented into words by ICTCLAS tools, thus the outputs to be combined can be seemed to have been segmented into words by ICTCLAS tools. While $\text{Joshua}_{\text{STANFORD}}$ represent the Joshua system that Chinese sentences in the training data have been segmented into words by STANFORD tool. Because the outputs to be combined have been segmented into words with different granularity, we must consistently re-segment the outputs into words or characters before system combination. The "ICTCLAS", and "STANFORD" rows show the scores when the system outputs are re-segmented into words by the respective Chinese word segmenters. Compared to word-level combination systems, "ICTCLAS", and "STANFORD", the character-level combination system, "Character", significantly improves the translation performance.

TABLE 2-The performance of word-level combination systems and character-level combination system on IWSLT'08 CRR EC task when Chinese translation outputs are originally segmented with different word granularity

	DEV					TST				
	BLEU	NIST	METEOR	GTM	TER	BLEU	NIST	METEOR	GTM	TER
$Joshua_{ICTCLAS}$	**76.02**	11.12	**80.10**	87.91	**18.82**	**48.34**	**7.50**	**62.34**	**76.98**	36.70
$Joshua_{STANFORD}$	76.00	**11.14**	79.82	**87.99**	18.89	47.81	7.44	61.94	76.60	**36.27**
ICTCLAS	76.29	11.02	79.01	87.55	19.26	49.29	7.43	62.31	76.94	36.27
STANFORD	76.23	11.23	79.82	87.87	18.97	48.96	7.54	62.12	77.29	36.20
Character	**76.68**	**11.23**	**80.32**	**88.44**	**18.81**	**49.59**	**7.63**	**63.51**	**77.55**	**35.69**

TABLE 3-The performance of word-level combination systems and character-level combination system on IWSLT'08 CRR EC task when Chinese translation outputs are originally segmented by the same CWS tool

	DEV					TST				
	BLEU	NIST	METEOR	GTM	TER	BLEU	NIST	METEOR	GTM	TER
$Moses_{ICTCLAS}$	75.43	11.02	79.38	87.33	19.46	46.24	7.26	61.56	76.33	37.10
$Joshua_{ICTCLAS}$	**76.02**	**11.12**	**80.10**	**87.91**	**18.82**	**48.34**	**7.50**	**62.34**	**76.98**	**36.70**
ICTCLAS	77.01	11.27	80.80	88.51	18.89	48.48	7.57	62.91	77.67	37.03
Character	**77.51**	**11.30**	**80.81**	**88.73**	**18.59**	**48.97**	**7.59**	**63.60**	**77.72**	**36.49**

When the outputs to be combined are generated by the SMT systems, $Moses_{ICTCLAS}$, and $Joshua_{ICTCLAS}$, in which the Chinese sentences in the training data have been segmented into words by the same CWS tool ICTCLAS, TABLE 3 shows the character-level combination system still consistently outperforms the word-level combination system even though the translation outputs to be combined are with the same word granularity.

Conclusion and discussion

In this paper, we conducted a detailed study of character-level versus word-level confusion network based system combination for Chinese translation output. The experimental results on NIST'08 EC tasks and IWSLT'08 EC CRR challenge tasks show that character-level combination system significantly outperforms word-level combination systems.

There are two possible reasons for character-level combination system better than word-level combination systems. First, Chinese sentences can be split into characters with perfect accuracy; however, there is not a CWS tool to perform 100% yet. Therefore, outputs can be segmented into characters more consistently, which lead to generate high quality monolingual hypothesis alignment to help construct confusion network. Secondarily, Chinese character is a smaller unit than Chinese word (containing at least one character) for constructing confusion network. Thus, character-level confusion network based system combination has more choice to produce better consensus translation.

Acknowledgments

This research has been funded by the Natural Science Foundation of China under Grant No. 6120 3313, 6127 2212, and 6116 3006, and also supported by the Natural Science Foundation of Jiangxi Educational Committee of China under Grant No. GJJ12212.

References

Banerjee, S., & Lavie, A. (2005). METEOR: An Automatic Metric for MT Evaluation with Improved Correlation with Human Judgments. In *Proceedings of the ACL Workshop on Intrinsic and Extrinsic Evaluation Measures for Machine Translation and/or Summarization.*

Chang, P.-C., Galley, M., & Manning, C. D. (2008). Optimizing Chinese Word Segmentation for Machine Translation Performance. In *Proceedings of the Third Workshop on Statistical Machine Translation.*

Chen, B., Zhang, M., Li, H., & Aw, A. (2009). A Comparative Study of Hypothesis Alignment and its Improvement for Machine Translation System Combination. In *Proceedings of ACL 2009.*

Doddington, G. (2002). Automatic Evaluation of Machine Translation Quality Using N-gram Co-occurrence Statistics. In *Proceedings of HLT 02.*

Du, J. (2011). Character-Level System Combination: An Empirical Study for English-to-Chinese Spoken Language Translation. In *International Conference on Asian Language Processing.*

Feng, Y., Liu, Y., Mi, H., Liu, Q., & Lv, Y. (2009). Lattice-based System Combination for Statistical Machine Translation. In *Proceedings of EMNLP 2009.*

He, X., Yang, M., Gao, J., Nguyen, P., & Moore, R. (2008). Indirect-HMM-based Hypothesis Alignment for Combining Outputs from Machine Translation Systems. In *Proceedings of EMNLP 2008.*

Koehn, P., Federico, M., Shen, W., Bertoldi, N., Bojar, O. r., Callison-Burch, C., et al. (2006). Open Source Toolkit for Statistical Machine Translation: Factored Translation Models and Confusion Network Decoding. In *John Hopkins University Summer Workshop.*

Li, C.-H., He, X., Liu, Y., & Xi, N. (2009). Incremental HMM Alignment for MT System Combination. In *Processing of ACL 2009.*

Li, M., Zong, C., & Ng, H. T. (2011). Automatic Evaluation of Chinese Translation Output: Word-Level or Character-Level? In *Processing of ACL 2011.*

Li, Z., Callison-Burch, C., Dyer, C., Ganitkevitch, J., Khudanpur, S., Schwartz, L., et al. (2009). Joshua: An Open Source Toolkit for Parsing-based Machine Translation. In *Proceedings of WMT 2009.*

Liu, C., Dahlmeier, D., & Ng, H. T. (2011). Better Evaluation Metrics Lead to Better Machine Translation. In *Proceedings of EMNLP 2011.*

Matusov, E., Ueffing, N., & Ney, H. (2006). Computing Consensus Translation from Multiple Machine Translation Systems Using Enhanced Hypotheses Alignment. In *Proceedings of EACL.*

Melamed, I. D., Green, R., & Turian, J. P. (2003). Precision and Recall of Machine Translation. In *Proceedings of HLT-NAACL 2003.*

Och, F. J., & Ney, H. (2003). A Systematic Comparison of Various Statistical Alignment Models. Computational Linguistics, 29(1), 19-51.

Papineni, K., Roukos, S., Ward, T., & Zhu, W.-J. (2002). BLEU: a Method for Automatic Evaluation of Machine Translation. In *Proceedings of ACL 2002.*

Paul, M. (2008). Overview of the IWSLT 2008 Evaluation Campaign. In *Proceedings of IWSLT 2008.*

Rosti, A.-V. I., Matsoukas, S., & Schwartz, R. (2007). Improved Word-Level System Combination for Machine Translation. In *Proceedings of ACL 2007.*

Snover, M., Dorr, B., Schwartz, R., Makhoul, J., Micciulla, L., & Makhoul, R. (2006). A Study of Translation Edit Rate with Targeted Human Annotation. In *Proceedings of AMTA 2006.*

Tseng, H., Chang, P., Andrew, G., Jurafsky, D., & Manning, C. (2005). A Conditional Random Field Word Segmenter for Sighan Bakeoff 2005. In *Proceedings of the Fourth SIGHAN Workshop on Chinese Language Processing.*

Wang, K., Zong, C., & Su, K.-Y. (2010). A Character-Based Joint Model for Chinese Word Segmentation. In *Proceedings of Coling 2010.*

Watanabe, T., & Sumita, E. (2011). Machine Translation System Combination by Confusion Forest. In *Proceedings of ACL 2011.*

Xu, J., Zens, R., & Ney, H. (2004). Do We Need Chinese Word Segmentation for Statistical Machine Translation? In *Proceedings of ACL-SIGHAN Workshop 2004.*

Zhang, H.-P., Liu, Q., Cheng, X.-Q., Zhang, H., & Yu, H.-K. (2003). Chinese Lexical Analysis Using Hierarchical Hidden Markov Model. In *Proceedings of the Second SIGHAN Workshop on Chinese Language Processing.*

Zhang, R., Yasuda, K., & Sumita, E. (2008). Chinese Word Segmentation and Statistical Machine Translation. ACM Transactions on Speech and Language Processing, 5(2), 1-19.

Using Cross-Lingual Explicit Semantic Analysis for Improving Ontology Translation

Kartik Asooja[1] *Jorge Gracia*[1]
Nitish Aggarwal[2] *Asunción Gómez Pérez*[1]
(1) Ontology Engineering Group, UPM, Madrid, Spain
(2) DERI, NUIG, Galway, Ireland
asooja@gmail.com, jgracia@fi.upm.es, nitish.aggarwal@deri.org, asun@fi.upm.es

Abstract

Semantic Web aims to allow machines to make inferences using the explicit conceptualisations contained in ontologies. By pointing to ontologies, Semantic Web-based applications are able to inter-operate and share common information easily. Nevertheless, multilingual semantic applications are still rare, owing to the fact that most online ontologies are monolingual in English. In order to solve this issue, techniques for ontology localisation and translation are needed. However, traditional machine translation is difficult to apply to ontologies, owing to the fact that ontology labels tend to be quite short in length and linguistically different from the free text paradigm. In this paper, we propose an approach to enhance machine translation of ontologies based on exploiting the well-structured concept descriptions contained in the ontology. In particular, our approach leverages the semantics contained in the ontology by using Cross Lingual Explicit Semantic Analysis (CLESA) for context-based disambiguation in phrase-based Statistical Machine Translation (SMT). The presented work is novel in the sense that application of CLESA in SMT has not been performed earlier to the best of our knowledge.

Keywords: Ontology Translation, Word-Sense Disambiguation, Statistical Machine translation, Explicit Semantic Analysis, Ontology Localisation.

1 Introduction

An ontology is a formal specification of a shared conceptualization (Gruber, 1993). Since the rise of Semantic Web, many ontology-based applications have been developed, for instance in the fields of ontology-based information extraction (Buitelaar et al., 2008), semantic search (Fernandez et al., 2008) and cross lingual information extraction (Embley et al., 2011). Nevertheless, due to the fact that most of the ontologies have been documented only in English and multilingual ontologies are rare, semantic applications that exploit information across natural language barriers are uncommon. In order to cross such barriers, a critical mass of multilingual ontologies is needed, as well as methods and techniques for ontology localisation and translation. In fact, ontology localisation, or the adaptation of an ontology to a particular language and culture (Espinoza et al., 2008a) has been identified as one of the key challenges of the multilingual Semantic Web (Gracia et al., 2012).

Translation of an ontology documented in a source language into target language is one of the most important steps in ontology localisation. Translating the ontology affects the lexical layer of an ontology. This layer includes all the natural language description including labels, comments, definitions, and associated documentation to make that ontology understandable for humans (Cimiano et al., 2010).

Ideally, ontology translation has to be supported by automatic methods, as finding domain experts knowing many languages is very difficult and expensive. It can be achieved by using machine translation (MT) techniques. Unfortunately, the labels in the ontologies pose extra challenges for standard practices in MT because of the different linguistic structure and short text length of the ontology labels compared to the free text paradigm (McCrae et al., 2011). In fact, ontology labels need not to be fully grammatically-correct sentences. Thus, a single ontology label typically constitutes a poor context to disambiguate the candidate translations of a lexical entry contained in that label.

It has been shown that performing word sense disambiguation (WSD) using the surrounding words for disambiguating the possible translations improve machine translation (Carpuat and Wu, 2007) (Chan et al., 2007). Following a similar intuition, such context disambiguation can also be applied to the translation of ontologies (Espinoza et al., 2008a). In that case, the ontology concepts are precisely defined and related to other concepts. Thus, the context of a concept can be enriched with the labels and textual descriptions of its connected concepts, and such context can be exploited for semantic disambiguation.

Therefore, we want to leverage the context from the ontology for improving the translation of labels. In this work, we use Cross Lingual Explicit Semantic Analysis (CLESA) based context disambiguation between the ontology context and the translation candidates, to rank the candidates, in the phrase-based Statistical Machine Translation (SMT) architecture. In our experiments, we use the labels of the connected entities of the source label in the ontology as the ontological context for any lexical entry, which comes from the source label.

This paper describes an approach that exploits ontological context from the ontology for improving automatic translation of the ontology labels. In particular, we have investigated the use of CLESA in SMT for this purpose. The remainder of this paper is structured as follows: Section 2 discusses some background required for better understanding of the rest of the paper. Section 3 describes the approach for using CLESA based WSD in SMT for ontology translation. Section 4 explains the evaluation setup and reports the experimental results. Section 5 describes some related work about the translation of ontologies. Finally, conclusions and future work are reported in the final section of the paper.

2 Background

In order to allow a better understanding of the rest of the paper, we briefly introduce here some basic notions of the techniques used in our approach.

2.1 Statistical Machine Translation

The statistical machine translation model utilizes the standard source-channel approach for statistically modeling the translation problem (Koehn et al., 2003) as follows:

$$argmax_{tgt} P(tgt|src) = argmax_{tgt} P(src|tgt)\ P_{LangModel}(tgt) \quad (1)$$

In equation 1, src and tgt refer to the source phrase and translated phrase respectively. The heuristic-based search is performed by the machine translation decoder to deduce the translation candidate with the maximum probability given the source phrase.

Phrase-based models generally perform better than word-based models as the phrase-based model tries to learn more of the local context and reduces the restrictions of word-based translation by translating whole sequences of words (Koehn et al., 2003). The phrases here are a sequence of words with all possible n-grams rather than only the linguistically correct phrases.

2.2 Cross Lingual Explicit Semantic Analysis

Explicit Semantic Analysis (ESA) was introduced by (Gabrilovich and Markovitch, 2007), and allows the semantic comparison of two texts with the help of explicitly defined concepts. In contrast, other techniques such as Latent Semantic Analysis (Landauer and Foltz, 1998) and Latent Dirichlet Allocation (Blei et al., 2003) build unsupervised concepts considering the correlations of the terms in the data. ESA is an algebraic model in which the text is represented with a vector of the explicit concepts as dimensions. The magnitude of each dimension in the vector is the associativity weight of the text to that explicit concept/dimension. To quantify this associativity, the textual content related to the explicit concept/dimension is utilized. This weight can be calculated by considering different methods, for instance, tf-idf score. A possible way of defining concepts in ESA is by means of using the Wikipedia [1] titles as dimensions of the model and the corresponding articles for calculating the associativity weight (Gabrilovich and Markovitch, 2007), thus taking advantage of the vast coverage of the community-developed Wikipedia. A compelling characteristic of Wikipedia is the large collective knowledge available in multiple languages, which facilitates an extension of existing ESA for multiple languages called Cross-lingual

[1] http://www.wikipedia.org/

Explicit Semantic Analysis (CLESA) (Sorg and Cimiano, 2008). The articles in Wikipedia are linked together across language, and this cross-lingual linked structure can provide a mapping of a vector in one language to the other. Thus, Wikipedia provides the comparable corpus in different languages, which is required by CLESA.

To understand CLESA, lets take two terms t_s in source language and t_t in the target language. As a first step, a concept vector for t_s is created using the Wikipedia corpus in the source language. Similarly, the concept vector for t_t is created in the target language. Then, one of the concept vectors can be converted to the other language by using the cross-lingual mappings provided by Wikipedia. After obtaining both of the concept vectors in one language, the relatedness of the terms t_s and t_t can be calculated by using cosine product, similar to ESA. For better efficiency, we chose to make a multilingual index by composing poly-lingual Wikipedia articles using the cross-lingual mappings. In such a case, no conversion of the concept vector in one language to the other is required. It is possible by representing the Wikipedia concept with some unique name common to all languages such as, for instance, the Uniform Resource Identifier (URI) of the English Wikipedia.

3 CLESA with SMT for Translating Ontologies

SMT systems implicitly use the local context for a better lexical choice during the translation (Carpuat and Wu, 2005). Accordingly, it is natural to assume that a focused WSD system integrated with SMT system might produce better translations. We follow the direct incorporation of WSD into SMT system as a multi-word phrasal lexical disambiguation system (Carpuat and Wu, 2007).

The WSD probability score calculated by using CLESA is added as an additional feature in the log-linear translation model. The CLESA based score would depend on the ontology in which the source label lies and ergo, the context of the ontology would be used to disambiguate the translation candidates. Equation 2 shows the integration of WSD in the standard phrase-based MT.

$$argmax_{tgt} P(tgt|src,O) = argmax_{tgt} P_{Translation}(src|tgt) P_{LangModel}(tgt) P_{Semantic}(tgt|O) \quad (2)$$

Here, the computation of equation 2 requires a heuristic search by the decoder to seek the best translation given the ontology O and the source phrase. The factor $P_{Semantic}(tgt|O)$ provides the probability score for a translation candidate given the ontology. This score is found by calculating the CLESA based semantic relatedness between the ontological context and the translation candidates. There can be several possibilities for selecting the context from the ontology, including the option to use the structure of the ontology for disambiguation (Espinoza et al., 2008a). For our experiments, the ontological context consists of labels of the connected entities to the source label in the ontology. Thereupon, we take a bag of words used in all the labels of the ontology and build the concept vector for the ontology to compare it with the concept vector of the translation candidates. We have employed Stanford Phrasal library (Cer et al., 2010), which is a phrase-based SMT system, in our architecture. It easily allows the integration of new features into the decoding model along with the already available features in the library (Cer et al., 2010).

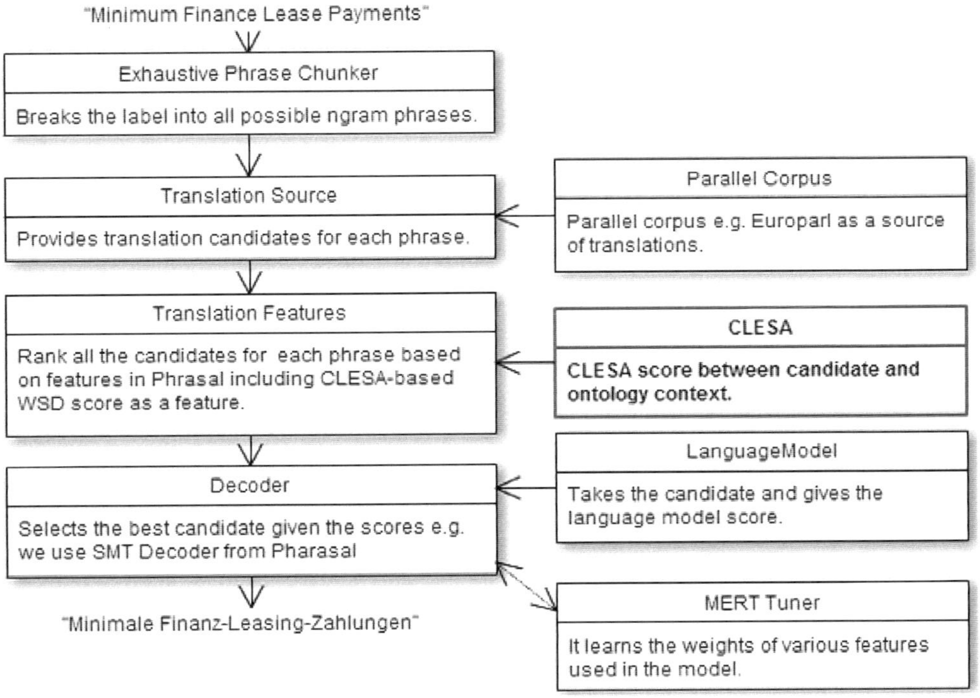

Figure 1: Phrase-based SMT architecture with CLESA integration.

Fig.1 shows the architecture applied for translating the ontologies. As an example, suppose that the SMT system has already been trained with some parallel corpus, for instance, Europarl corpus (Koehn, 2005). It receives an example English label "Minimum Finance Lease Payments" from a source ontology to translate it into German. The label is broken into a phrase chunk list containing all the possible phrases by the *Exhaustive Phrase Chunker*. As a next step, the *Translation Source* provides all the possible translation candidates for each phrase chunk in the chunk list. *Translation Source* can be a phrase table made from some parallel corpus like Europarl. Then, scores are assigned to all the translation candidates based on several standard *Translation Features* exisiting in the Phrasal library. As an additional feature, we introduce one more score based on the *CLESA* based semantic relevance of the candidate against the source ontology context, which includes all its labels. All these feature scores are combined by a log-linear model. The *MERT Tuner* (Och, 2003) is just used once to learn the weights of various features used in the model for a particular language pair. In the final step, the decoder performs search over all the translation candidates given the scores from *Translation Features* and the *Language Model*, and makes the German translation "Minimale Finanz-Leasing-Zahlungen".

For implementing CLESA, we followed an information retrieval based approach by creating a Lucene [2] inverted index of a Wikipedia dump from Jan, 2012. As a preprocessing step, all the Wikipedia namespace type articles such as mediaWiki, talk, help etc. were removed. For creating the weighted vector of concepts for a translation candidate in the

[2]http://lucene.apache.org/core/

target language, the term is searched over the Wikipedia index of the respective language to retrieve the top associated Wikipedia concepts and the Lucene ranking scores are taken as the associativity weights of the concepts to the term. We took the top 2000 Wikipedia concepts for our experiment as we found that increasing this number did not have any major effect on the translation metrics, but it significantly increases the computational time. As the ontological context for any phrase chunk, we use the source label along with the labels from the connected entities to the source label in the ontology. Thus, the concept vector for the ontological context is created by searching the ontological context in the Wikipedia index of the source language.

4 Evaluation

To evaluate the integration of CLESA in the SMT architecture, we perform the translation of several ontologies and compare the results, against reference translations, with the translations performed by a baseline SMT system. We used widely accepted machine translation metrics in our evaluation: WER (Popović and Ney, 2007), BLEU (Papineni et al., 2002), NIST(Doddington, 2002), METEOR (Banerjee and Lavie, 2005). All the translations were performed for English to Spanish, English to German and English to Dutch language pairs.

4.1 Experimental Setup

To build a baseline SMT system, we used the Stanford Phrasal library trained on EuroParl corpus (Koehn, 2005). In order to define our benchmark, we have used some multilingual ontologies available online (See table 1). For tuning the SMT system using MERT tuner, IFRS ontology was used as it contains 2757 labels (McCrae et al., 2011) for each language in the consideration, which is quite large against the number of labels present in the ontologies used for evaluation. We used a monolingual version of each ontology as input to the evaluation process. Then, we used the labels in the target language as reference translations and compared them to the translations obtained in the process. Finally, the evaluation metrics were computed. To test the effect of CLESA-based disambiguation in SMT, we run the experiments both with our SMT baseline system and with the CLESA integrated in the baseline system.

4.2 Results and Discussions

Tables 2, 3 and 4 show the results in our experiments for the English to German, English to Spanish and English to Dutch language pairs respectively.

We can see that the metric scores are low, which could be mainly because of lower word/phrase coverage. Although, the results show an improvement in BLEU-2, METEOR, NIST and WER (WER is better if the score is low) but not in BLEU-4. This is the result of the linguistic differences between free-text and ontology labels. Labels of an ontology generally tend to be shorter in length, therefore BLEU-2 (BLEU with 2-grams) gives better correlation with the reference translations than BLEU-4 (BLEU with 4-grams). It is probably because the average number of tokens is less than 4 in the evaluated ontologies. These metrics

Ontology	English	Spanish	German	Dutch
GeoSkills	211	46	238	360
Crop-Wild Relatives Ontology	1030	1025	0	0
FOAF	88	79	0	0
Housing Benefits	841	0	0	841
Open EHR Reference	36	36	0	0
Registratie Bedrijven	854	0	0	854
DOAP	47	36	35	0
ITCC CI 2011	417	0	417	0
Open EHR Demographics	24	24	0	0

Table 1: Multilingual Ontologies with the number of labels in the respective languages

Ontology		BLEU-4	BLEU-2	METEOR	NIST	WER
DOAP	Baseline	0.0	0.0	0.014	0.101	1.176
	CLESA	0.0	0.0	0.014	0.101	1.176
ITCC CI 2011	Baseline	0.0	0.022	0.043	0.791	1.070
	CLESA	0.0	0.022	0.044	0.802	1.068
GeoSkills	Baseline	0.0	0.0	0.032	0.509	1.214
	CLESA	0.0	0.0	0.034	0.523	1.209
Summary	Baseline	**0.0**	**0.014**	**0.038**	**0.669**	**1.118**
	CLESA	**0.0**	**0.014**	**0.039**	**0.680**	**1.117**

Table 2: Baseline and Baseline+CLESA scores for English to German

do not suit well to the task of ontology translation as they do in the free text paradigm (McCrae et al., 2011). Therefore, there is a need for the development of new metrics for evaluating the translation of ontologies.

From the result tables, we can see that the use of the CLESA ranker slightly improves the baseline results in most of the cases. The improvement is little because the integration of CLESA does not provide new translation candidates to the system, it just gives more weightage to the ones which are semantically more related to the ontological context.

5 Related Work

Label-Translator, developed as a NEON plug-in (Espinoza et al., 2008b), is one of the initial initiatives to automatically localize the ontology. It does not follow SMT-centered approach (Espinoza et al., 2008a). As a first step, it collects the candidate translations for a label by consulting different bilingual linguistic resources and translation services such as Google Translate. Then, it performs WSD by using the ontological context of the label against the candidates for selecting the best one. The context in which those candidates appear in different domains is taken from various multilingual ontologies and linguistic resources such as EuroWordnet (Vossen, 1998). One of the pre-requisites of Label-Translator is

Ontology		BLEU-4	BLEU-2	METEOR	NIST	WER
DOAP	Baseline	0.0	0.145	0.204	1.891	0.853
	CLESA	0.0	0.149	0.211	1.985	0.853
Open EHR Demographics	Baseline	0.0	0.0	0.095	0.736	1.028
	CLESA	0.0	0.0	0.095	0.736	1.028
CWR	Baseline	0.075	0.180	0.170	3.072	0.983
	CLESA	0.074	0.180	0.175	3.152	0.986
Open EHR Reference	Baseline	0.0	0.152	0.206	1.516	0.933
	CLESA	0.0	0.155	0.220	1.600	0.920
GeoSkills	Baseline	0.256	0.254	0.246	2.289	0.938
	CLESA	0.0	0.230	0.240	2.202	0.954
FOAF	Baseline	0.0	0.187	0.204	2.487	0.874
	CLESA	0.0	0.187	0.204	2.487	0.874
Summary	Baseline	**0.069**	**0.177**	**0.175**	**2.888**	**0.971**
	CLESA	**0.061**	**0.177**	**0.179**	**2.958**	**0.973**

Table 3: Baseline and Baseline+CLESA scores for English to Spanish

Ontology		BLEU-4	BLEU-2	METEOR	NIST	WER
Registratie Bedrijven	Baseline	0.0	0.113	0.112	1.540	0.955
	CLESA	0.0	0.113	0.113	1.550	0.954
Housing Benefits	Baseline	0.0	0.128	0.120	1.530	0.908
	CLESA	0.0	0.127	0.120	1.530	0.910
GeoSkills	Baseline	0.0	0.099	0.076	1.181	1.113
	CLESA	0.0	0.100	0.079	1.230	1.108
Summary	Baseline	**0.0**	**0.117**	**0.113**	**1.520**	**0.945**
	CLESA	**0.0**	**0.117**	**0.114**	**1.528**	**0.944**

Table 4: Baseline and Baseline+CLESA scores for English to Dutch

that it relies on the existence of the candidate translations in EuroWordNet (or similar resources) in order to operate. On the contrary, the CLESA-based approach does not suffer such limitation. Our approach does not, therefore, depend on the availability of external translation services. Furthermore, thanks to the wide language coverage of Wikipedia, the extension of the CLESA-based approach to other language pairs is straightforward.

The problem of translating ontologies has already been discussed in the context of SMT (McCrae et al., 2011), although, not much work has been done in actually experimenting with WSD in a SMT system for translating ontologies.

Therefore, we integrated CLESA into a phrase-based SMT architecture for translating labels of the ontologies. CLESA is shown to perform better than the latent concept models in the context of cross lingual information retrieval task (Cimiano et al., 2009), which motivated us to use it in SMT also.

Conclusion

We have presented an approach for ontology translation that uses CLESA for leveraging the ontological context in a Statistical Machine Translation process. Integration of CLESA based disambiguation using all the ontology labels in SMT architecture, provides the selection of the translation candidates given the ontological context, in contrast to the standard phrase-based model, which considers only the local context in the label. The results show little improvements over the baseline scores for most of the evaluation metrics, thus proving that exploring the ontology context based disambiguation may be beneficial in the process of translating the ontologies. Nevertheless, more research is needed in that direction in order to attain better results. As future work, we plan to investigate better ways of exploiting the ontological context for machine translation of labels and to compare our system against the Label-Translator.

Acknowledgements

This work is supported in part by the European Union under Grant No. 248458 for the Monnet project.

References

Banerjee, S. and Lavie, A. (2005). Meteor: An automatic metric for mt evaluation with improved correlation with human judgments. pages 65–72.

Blei, D. M., Ng, A. Y., and Jordan, M. I. (2003). Latent dirichlet allocation. *J. Mach. Learn. Res.*, 3:993–1022.

Buitelaar, P., Cimiano, P., Frank, A., Hartung, M., and Racioppa, S. (2008). Ontology-based information extraction and integration from heterogeneous data sources. *International Journal of Human Computer Studies (JHCS)*, 66:759–788.

Carpuat, M. and Wu, D. (2005). Evaluating the word sense disambiguation performance of statistical machine translation.

Carpuat, M. and Wu, D. (2007). Improving statistical machine translation using word sense disambiguation. In *In The 2007 Joint Conference on Empirical Methods in Natural Language Processing and Computational Natural Language Learning (EMNLP-CoNLL 2007*, pages 61–72.

Cer, D., Galley, M., Jurafsky, D., and Manning, C. D. (2010). Phrasal: a toolkit for statistical machine translation with facilities for extraction and incorporation of arbitrary model features. In *Proceedings of the NAACL HLT 2010 Demonstration Session*, HLT-DEMO '10, pages 9–12, Stroudsburg, PA, USA. Association for Computational Linguistics.

Chan, Y. S., Ng, H. T., and Chiang, D. (2007). Word sense disambiguation improves statistical machine translation. In *Proceedings of the 45th Annual Meeting of the Association of Computational Linguistics*, pages 33–40, Prague, Czech Republic. Association for Computational Linguistics.

Cimiano, P., Montiel-Ponsoda, E., Buitelaar, P., Espinoza, M., and Gómez-Pérez, A. (2010). A note on ontology localization. *Appl. Ontol.*, 5(2):127–137.

Cimiano, P., Schultz, A., Sizov, S., Sorg, P., and Staab, S. (2009). Explicit versus latent concept models for cross-language information retrieval. In *Proceedings of the 21st international jont conference on Artifical intelligence*, IJCAI'09, pages 1513–1518, San Francisco, CA, USA. Morgan Kaufmann Publishers Inc.

Doddington, G. (2002). Automatic evaluation of machine translation quality using n-gram co-occurrence statistics. In *Proceedings of the second international conference on Human Language Technology Research*, HLT '02, pages 138–145, San Francisco, CA, USA. Morgan Kaufmann Publishers Inc.

Embley, D. W., Liddle, S. W., Lonsdale, D. W., and Tijerino, Y. (2011). Multilingual ontologies for cross-language information extraction and semantic search. In *Proceedings of the 30th international conference on Conceptual modeling*, ER'11, pages 147–160, Berlin, Heidelberg. Springer-Verlag.

Espinoza, M., Gómez-Pérez, A., and Mena, E. (2008a). Enriching an ontology with multilingual information. In *Proceedings of the 5th European semantic web conference on The semantic web:research and applications*, ESWC'08, pages 333–347, Berlin, Heidelberg. Springer-Verlag.

Espinoza, M., Gómez-Pérez, A., and Mena, E. (2008b). Labeltranslator - a tool to automatically localize an ontology. In *Proceedings of the 5th European semantic web conference on The semantic web: research and applications*, ESWC 08, pages 792–796, Berlin, Heidelberg. Springer-Verlag.

Fernandez, M., Lopez, V., Sabou, M., Uren, V., Vallet, D., Motta, E., and Castells, P. (2008). Semantic search meets the web. In *Proceedings of the 2008 IEEE International Conference on Semantic Computing*, ICSC '08, pages 253–260, Washington, DC, USA. IEEE Computer Society.

Gabrilovich, E. and Markovitch, S. (2007). Computing semantic relatedness using wikipedia-based explicit semantic analysis. In *Proceedings of the 20th international joint conference on Artifical intelligence*, IJCAI'07, pages 1606–1611, San Francisco, CA, USA. Morgan Kaufmann Publishers Inc.

Gracia, J., Montiel-Ponsoda, E., Cimiano, P., Gómez-Pérez, A., Buitelaar, P., and McCrae, J. (2012). Challenges for the multilingual web of data. *Web Semant.*, 11:63–71.

Gruber, T. R. (1993). A translation approach to portable ontology specifications. *KNOWLEDGE ACQUISITION*, 5:199–220.

Koehn, P. (2005). Europarl: A Parallel Corpus for Statistical Machine Translation. In *Conference Proceedings: the tenth Machine Translation Summit*, pages 79–86, Phuket, Thailand. AAMT, AAMT.

Koehn, P., Och, F. J., and Marcu, D. (2003). Statistical phrase-based translation. In *Proceedings of the 2003 Conference of the North American Chapter of the Association for Computational Linguistics on Human Language Technology - Volume 1*, NAACL '03, pages 48–54, Stroudsburg, PA, USA. Association for Computational Linguistics.

Landauer, T. K. and Foltz, P. W. (1998). An Introduction To Latent Semantic Analysis.

McCrae, J., Espinoza, M., Montiel-Ponsoda, E., Aguado-de Cea, G., and Cimiano, P. (2011). Combining statistical and semantic approaches to the translation of ontologies and taxonomies. In *Proceedings of the Fifth Workshop on Syntax, Semantics and Structure in Statistical Translation*, SSST-5, pages 116–125, Stroudsburg, PA, USA. Association for Computational Linguistics.

Och, F. J. (2003). Minimum error rate training in statistical machine translation. In *Proceedings of the 41st Annual Meeting on Association for Computational Linguistics - Volume 1*, ACL '03, pages 160–167, Stroudsburg, PA, USA. Association for Computational Linguistics.

Papineni, K., Roukos, S., Ward, T., and jing Zhu, W. (2002). Bleu: a method for automatic evaluation of machine translation. pages 311–318.

Popović, M. and Ney, H. (2007). Word error rates: decomposition over pos classes and applications for error analysis. In *Proceedings of the Second Workshop on Statistical Machine Translation*, StatMT '07, pages 48–55, Stroudsburg, PA, USA. Association for Computational Linguistics.

Sorg, P. and Cimiano, P. (2008). Cross-lingual information retrieval with explicit semantic analysis. In *Working Notes for the CLEF 2008 Workshop*.

Vossen, P., editor (1998). *EuroWordNet: a multilingual database with lexical semantic networks*. Kluwer Academic Publishers, Norwell, MA, USA.

System Combination with Extra Alignment Information

Xiaofeng Wu   Tsyoshi Okita   Josef van Genabith   Qun Liu
Centre of Next Generation Localisation(CNGL), School of Computing, Dublin City University
{xiaofengwu,tokita,josef,qliu}@computing.dcu.ie

ABSTRACT
This paper provides the system description of the IHMM team of Dublin City University for our participation in the system combination task in the Second Workshop on Applying Machine Learning Techniques to Optimise the Division of Labour in Hybrid MT (ML4HMT-12). Our work is based on a confusion network-based approach to system combination. We propose a new method to build a confusion network for this: (1) incorporate extra alignment information extracted from given meta data, treating them as sure alignments, into the results from IHMM, and (2) decode together with this information. We also heuristically set one of the system outputs as the default backbone. Our results show that this backbone, which is the RBMT system output, achieves an 0.11% improvement in BLEU over the backbone chosen by TER, while the extra information we added in the decoding part does not improve the results.

KEYWORDS: system combination, confusion network, indirect HMM alignment, backbone chosen.

1 Introduction

This paper describes a new extension to our system combination module in Dublin City University for the participation in the system combination task in the ML4HMT-2012 workshop. We incorporate alignment meta information to the alignment module when building a confusion network.

Given multiple translation outputs, a system combination strategy aims at finding the best translations, either by choosing one sentence or generating a new translation from fragments originated from individual systems(Banerjee et al., 2010). Combination methods have been widely used in fields such as parsing (Henderson and Brill, 1999) and speech recognition (Fiscus, 1997). In late the 90s, the speech recognition community produced a confusion network-based system combination approach, spreading instantly to SMT community as well.

The traditional system combination approach employs confusion networks which are built by the monolingual alignment which induces sentence similarity. Confusion networks are compact graph-based structures representing multiple hypothesises (Bangalore et al., 2001). It is noted that there are several generalized forms of confusion networks as well. One is a lattice (Feng et al., 2009) and the other is a translation forest (Watanabe and Sumita, 2011). The former employs lattices that can describe arbitrary mappings in hypothesis alignments. A lattice is more general than a confusion network. By contrast, a confusion forest exploits syntactic similarity between individual outputs.

Up to now, various state-of-the-art alignment methods have been developed including Indirect-HMM (He et al., 2008; Du and Way, 2010) which is a statistical-model-based method, and TER which is a metric-based method which uses an edit distance. In this work we focus on the IHMM method.

The main problem of IHMM is that there are numerous one-to-many and one-to-null cases in the alignment results. This alignment noise significantly affects the confusion network construction and the decoding process. In this work, in addition to the IHMM alignment, we also incorporate alignment meta information extracted from an RBMT system to help the decoding process.

The other crucial factor is the backbone selection which also affects the combination results. The backbone determines the word order in the final output. Backbone selection is often done by Minimum Bayes Risk (MBR) decoding which selects a hypothesis with minimum average distance among all hypotheses (Rosti et al., 2007a,b). In this work we heuristically choose an RBMT output as the backbone due to its (expected) overall grammatically well-formed output and better human evaluation results.

We report our results and provide a comparison with traditional confusion-network-based network approach.

The remainder of the paper is organized as follows: We will review the state-of-the-art system combination framework based on confusion networks in Section 2. We describe our experimental setup, how we extract the alignment information from meta-data and how we use it in Section 3. The results and analysis are also given in this section. We draw conclusions in Section 4.

Figure 1: Word level confusion network based system combination architecture

H_1: He jogs in the park
H_2: He runs the park
H_3: Garden he runs
H_4: It in garden

(a)

He	jogs	in	ε	the	park
He	runs	ε	ε	the	park
he	runs	ε	ε	ε	Garden
it	ε	in	ε	ε	garden

(b)

Figure 2: a) The hypothesises collected; (b) the final confusion net work constructed.

2 Background on Confusion Networks

2.1 Confusion Network Architecture

The current state-of-art approach to word level system combination is described in (Rosti et al., 2007b). The system architecture is illustrated in Figure 1.

Suppose we have collected four system outputs H_1-H_4 which are shown in Figure 2a. Then the traditional way of choosing a backbone is to use minimum average edit distance (or other measurements) as shown in Equation 1.

$$B = H^* = argmin_{H \in \nabla} \sum_{H \in \nabla} (H_i, H) \tag{1}$$

The backbone is used to decide the word order of the final output. After obtaining the backbone, all other hypotheses are aligned to it. The alignment strategies include IHMM, TER, etc. Note that during the word alignment word reordering and 'null' insertion are performed, which is usually called normalization. The confusion network, which can be constructed directly from the normalized alignment is given in Figure 2b, in which case H_1 is chosen as the backbone.

2.2 Indirect HMM Alignment

In this work we implement the IHMM (He et al., 2008). IHMM is a refined version of HMM alignment (Vogel et al., 1996) which is widely used in bilingual word alignment (Och and Ney, 2003).

Let $B = (b_1, ..., b_J)$ denote the J words in the backbone sentence, $H = (h_1, ..., h_I)$ denote one of the hypothesis, and $A = (a_1, ..., a_J)$ denote the alignment of each backbone word to the hypothesis word. We use Equation 2 to compute the alignment probability of each word pair. In Equation 2, d represents the distortion model and p denotes the word similarity model.

$$P(H|B) = \sum_{A} \prod_{j=1...J} [d(a_j|a_{j-1}, I)p(h_j|b_{a_j})] \tag{2}$$

In order to handle the words which are aligned to an empty word, we also insert a *null* associated with each backbone word.

We follow (Vogel et al., 1996) and use Equation 3 to compute the distortion model.

$$d(i|i',I) = \frac{c(i-i')}{\sum_{l=1}^{I} c(l-i)} \tag{3}$$

Where $c(\Delta)$ represents the word distance grouped into $c(\leq -4), c(-3), ..., c(0), ..., c(5), c(\geq 6)$ 13 buckets, and computed with Equation 4 which peak at $\Delta = 1$.

$$c(\Delta) = (1 + |\Delta - 1|)^{-2} \tag{4}$$

The word similarity probability in Equation 2 is computed by Equation 5. We use two small Chinese-English & English-Chinese dictionaries (10k entries each) to compute $p_{semantic}$, and the longest common subsequence matching score to obtain $p_{surface}$.

$$p(h_j|b_i) = \alpha p_{semantic}(h_j|b_i) + (1-\alpha) p_{surface}(h_j|b_i) \tag{5}$$

Given an HMM model, we use the Viterbi algorithm to obtain the one-to-many alignment, and by reordering and inserting *null* to their proper position both in the backbone and hypothesis, the final normalized alignment are produced, as shown in Figure 2b.

2.3 Decoding & Parameter tuning

We use a log linear combination strategy shown in Equation 6, which is described in (Rosti et al., 2007a), to compute the hypothesis confidence.

$$logp(E|F) = \sum_{i=1}^{N_{nodes}-1} log(\sum_{i=1}^{N_{system}} w_l p(word|l,i)) + \nu Lm(E) + \mu N_{nulls}(E) + \epsilon Len(E) \tag{6}$$

where N_{nodes} is the number of nodes the current confusion network has, N_{system} is the number of sytems, w denotes the system weight, *Lm* represents the language model score of the current path, N_{nulls} stands for the number of nulls inserted, and Len is the length of the current path. ν ,μ and ϵ are the corresponding weights of each feature.

A beam search algorithm is employed to find the best path.

3 Experimental Setup

3.1 Data

We participate in the ML4HMT-12 shared task ES-EN. Participants are given a development bilingual data set aligned at the sentence level. Each "bilingual sentence" contains: 1) the source sentence, 2) the target (reference) sentence and 3) the corresponding multiple output translations from four systems, based on different MT approaches (Ramırez-Sánchez et al., 2006; Alonso and Thurmair, 2003; Koehn et al., 2007). The output has been annotated with system-internal meta-data information derived from the translation process of each of the systems.

In this work we use 1000 sentence pair from the 10K development set to tune the system parameters and all the 3003 sentence pairs in the test set to run the test.

3.2 Backbone Selection

Equation 1 describes the traditional backbone selection. However in this work we heuristically set Lucy RBMT (Alonso and Thurmair, 2003) output as the backbone. Our motivations are that: 1) Lucy's output tends to be more grammatical than Moses or other MT systems; 2) according to the previous ML4HMT-2011, Lucy has better human evaluation scores than other statistical machine translation systems.

3.3 Alignment Extraction of Lucy

The Lucy LT RBMT (Alonso and Thurmair, 2003) takes three steps to translate a source language string into a target language string: an analysis step, a transfer step, and a generation step. The meta data annotations provided in ML4HMT development set follows these three steps describing the parse tree for the respective translation steps.

We extract the alignment from this annotation in the following manner. First, we extract tuples where each connects a source word, intermediate words, and a target word by looking at the annotation file. There are some alignments dropped in this process. Such dropped alignments include the alignment of UNK (unknown)words marked by the Lucy LT RBMT system, words such as "do" which will not appear in the transfer step, and so forth. One remark is that since we trace these annotations based on the parse tree structure provided by the Lucy LT RBMT system, the exact order in the sentence is sometimes lost. This caused a problem when there are multiple "the", "of", and so forth, tokens in the string, so that for a given "the" in sources there are multiple target position. Second, we delete the intermediate representations, and obtain the source and the target words/phrases pairs.

Examples of the extracted alignments (the second sentence in test set) are shown in Figure 3.

From Figure 3 we can see that words like 'últimos' which has a one-to-one alignment are all correct alignments, while words like 'de' or 'el' which are involved in many-to-many alignment, carry much less confidence for the alignment. Given this observation, one idea would be using these extracted sure alignments, which are one-to-one, to guide decoding.

3.4 Decoding with Alignment Bias

In the decoding part, we change the Equation 6 into Equation 7 as follows

$$p(E_\psi) = \theta_\psi logp(E_\psi|F) \tag{7}$$

where $\psi = 1...N_{nodes}$ denotes the current node at which the beam search arrived, and $\theta_\psi = 1$ if a current node is not a sure alignment extracted from Lucy's meta-data and $\theta_\psi > 1$, otherwise.

```
TGT:the(0) period(1) aktuálně.cz(2) "(3) examined(4) "(5) the(6) members(7) of(8) the(9)
new(10) board(11) of(12) the(13) čssd(14) to(15) check(16) its(17) knowledge(18) of(19) the(20)
language(21) marked(22) slang(23) that(24) has(25) risen(26) up(27) in(28) the(29) last(30)
years(31) in(32) the(33) board(34) ,(35) when(36) the(37) current(38) members(39) of(40) the(41)
coalition(42) governed(43) prague(44) .(45)
SRC:El(0) período(1) Aktuálně.cz(2) "(3) examinó(4) "(5) a(6) los(7) miembros(8) del(9) nuevo(10)
Consejo(11) del(12) ČSSD(13) para(14) comprobar(15) sus(16) conocimientos(17) del(18) lengua(19)
marcado(20) slang(21) que(22) ha(23) surgido(24) en(25) los(26) últimos(27) años(28) en(29) el(30)
Consejo(31) ,(32) cuando(33) gobernaban(34) Praga(35) los(36) actuales(37) miembros(38) de(39)
la(40) coalición(41) .(42)
2 ||| [[u'el'], [[30]], [u'the'], [[0, 6, 9, 13, 20, 29, 33, 37, 41]]]
2 ||| [[u'per\xedodo'], [[1]], [u'period'], [[1]]]
2 ||| [[u'examin\xf3'], [[4]], [u'examined'], [[4]]]
2 ||| [[u'a'], [[6]], [u'to'], [[15]]]
2 ||| [[u'los'], [[7, 26, 36]], [u'the'], [[0, 6, 9, 13, 20, 29, 33, 37, 41]]]
2 ||| [[u'miembros'], [[8, 38]], [u'members'], [[7, 39]]]
2 ||| [[u'de'], [[39]], [u'of'], [[8, 12, 19, 40]]]
2 ||| [[u'l'], ['-1'], [u'the'], [[0, 6, 9, 13, 20, 29, 33, 37, 41]]]
2 ||| [[u'nuevo'], [[10]], [u'new'], [[10]]]
2 ||| [[u'consejo'], [[11, 31]], [u'Board'], [[11, 34]]]
2 ||| [[u'comprobar'], [[15]], [u'check'], [[16]]]
2 ||| [[u'sus'], [[16]], [u'its'], [[17]]]
2 ||| [[u'conocimientos'], [[17]], [u'knowledge'], [[18]]]
2 ||| [[u'lengua'], [[19]], [u'language'], [[21]]]
2 ||| [[u'surgido'], [[24]], [u'risen'], [[26]]]
2 ||| [[u'en'], [[25, 29]], [u'in'], [[28, 32]]]
2 ||| [[u'\xfaltimos'], [[27]], [u'last'], [[30]]]
2 ||| [[u'a\xf1os'], [[28]], [u'years'], [[31]]]
2 ||| [[u'cuando'], [[33]], [u'when'], [[36]]]
2 ||| [[u'gobernaban'], [[34]], [u'governed'], [[43]]]
2 ||| [[u'Praga'], [[35]], [u'Prague'], [[44]]]
2 ||| [[u'actuales'], [[37]], [u'current'], [[38]]]
2 ||| [[u'la'], [[40]], [u'the'], [[0, 6, 9, 13, 20, 29, 33, 37, 41]]]
2 ||| [[u'coalici\xf3n'], [[41]], [u'coalition'], [[42]]]
```

Figure 3: extracted alignment from Lucy LT RBMT meta data.

3.5 Experimental Results and Analysis

In our experiments, we set α 0.1 in Equation 5, according to (Feng et al., 2009). All development set and test set data are tokenized and lower cased. We use mteval-v13.pl[1], no-smoothing and case sensitive for the evaluation.

Table 1 shows the result of using Lucy as a backbone and the result of changing θ_ψ on the development and test sets. Note that $\theta_\psi = 1$ stands for the case when there is no effect of this factor on the current path.

θ_ψ	Devset(1000)		Testset(3003)	
	NIST	BLEU	NIST	BLEU
1	8.1328	0.3376	7.4546	0.2607
1.2	8.1179	0.3355	7.2109	0.2597
1.5	8.1171	0.3355	7.4512	0.2578
2	8.1252	0.3360	7.4532	0.2558
4	8.1180	0.3354	7.3540	0.2569
10	8.1190	0.3354	7.1026	0.2557

Table 1: The Lucy backbone with tuning of θ_ψ.

From Table 1, we see a slight decrease of quanlity when we increased the factor. But an

[1] ftp://jaguar.ncsl.nist.gov/mt/resources/mteval-v13.pl

interesting observation is that when we increased θ_ψ to 10 the result was not much affected. We believe this is since the sure alignments which we extracted from the Lucy alignments were almost perfectly consistent with the alignment resulting from IHMM. The best path derived by IHMM included most of the sure alignments extracted from Lucy.

	Devset(1000)		Testset(3003)	
TER Backbone	8.1168	0.3351	7.1092	0.2596
Lucy Backbone	8.1328	0.3376	7.4546	0.2607

Table 2: TER Backbone selection results.

We compared results with thos obtained by Lucy backbone (which are in the Table 1 when $\theta_\psi = 1$) with that of the TER backbone in Table 2. We can see that the Lucy backbone result was 0.11% better than that of TER. This confirmed our assumption that Lucy would be a good backbone in system combination.

4 Conclusion

In this paper we describe new approaches we applied in building a confusion network. We focus on backbone selection and adding extra alignment information. Our results show that with choosing Lucy, which is an RBMT system, as a backbone the result is slightly better (0.11% improvment by BLEU) than the traditional TER backbone selection method. However the extra alignment information we added in the decoding part does not improve the performance. In our future work we will further analyse the reason for this.

Acknowledgments

This work was supported by Science Foundation Ireland (Grant No. 07/CE/I1142) as part of the Centre for Next Generation Localisation (www.cngl.ie) at Dublin City University.

References

Alonso, J. and Thurmair, G. (2003). The comprendium translator system. In *Proceedings of the Ninth Machine Translation Summit*.

Banerjee, P., Du, J., Li, B., Kumar Naskar, S., Way, A., and Van Genabith, J. (2010). Combining multi-domain statistical machine translation models using automatic classifiers. Association for Machine Translation in the Americas.

Bangalore, B., Bordel, G., and Riccardi, G. (2001). Computing consensus translation from multiple machine translation systems. In *Automatic Speech Recognition and Understanding, 2001. ASRU'01. IEEE Workshop on*, pages 351–354. IEEE.

Du, J. and Way, A. (2010). Using terp to augment the system combination for smt. Association for Machine Translation in the Americas.

Feng, Y., Liu, Y., Mi, H., Liu, Q., and Lü, Y. (2009). Lattice-based system combination for statistical machine translation. In *Proceedings of the 2009 Conference on Empirical Methods in Natural Language Processing: Volume 3-Volume 3*, pages 1105–1113. Association for Computational Linguistics.

Fiscus, J. (1997). A post-processing system to yield reduced word error rates: Recognizer output voting error reduction (rover). In *Automatic Speech Recognition and Understanding, 1997. Proceedings., 1997 IEEE Workshop on*, pages 347–354. IEEE.

He, X., Yang, M., Gao, J., Nguyen, P., and Moore, R. (2008). Indirect-hmm-based hypothesis alignment for combining outputs from machine translation systems. In *Proceedings of the Conference on Empirical Methods in Natural Language Processing*, pages 98–107. Association for Computational Linguistics.

Henderson, J. and Brill, E. (1999). Exploiting diversity in natural language processing: Combining parsers. In *Proceedings of the Fourth Conference on Empirical Methods in Natural Language Processing*, pages 187–194.

Koehn, P., Hoang, H., Birch, A., Callison-Burch, C., Federico, M., Bertoldi, N., Cowan, B., Shen, W., Moran, C., Zens, R., et al. (2007). Moses: Open source toolkit for statistical machine translation. In *Annual meeting-association for computational linguistics*, volume 45, page 2.

Och, F. and Ney, H. (2003). A systematic comparison of various statistical alignment models. *Computational linguistics*, 29(1):19–51.

Ramırez-Sánchez, G., Sánchez-Martınez, F., Ortiz-Rojas, S., Pérez-Ortiz, J., and Forcada, M. (2006). Opentrad apertium open-source machine translation system: an opportunity for business and research. In *Proceedings of the Twenty-Eighth International Conference on Translating and the Computer*. Citeseer.

Rosti, A., Ayan, N., Xiang, B., Matsoukas, S., Schwartz, R., and Dorr, B. (2007a). Combining outputs from multiple machine translation systems. In *Human Language Technologies 2007: The Conference of the North American Chapter of the Association for Computational Linguistics*, pages 228–235.

Rosti, A., Matsoukas, S., and Schwartz, R. (2007b). Improved word-level system combination for machine translation. In *ANNUAL MEETING-ASSOCIATION FOR COMPUTATIONAL LINGUISTICS*, volume 45, page 312.

Vogel, S., Ney, H., and Tillmann, C. (1996). Hmm-based word alignment in statistical translation. In *Proceedings of the 16th conference on Computational linguistics-Volume 2*, pages 836–841. Association for Computational Linguistics.

Watanabe, T. and Sumita, E. (2011). Machine translation system combination by confusion forest. In *Proceedings of the 49th Annual Meeting of the Association for Computational Linguistics: Human Language Technologies-Volume 1*, pages 1249–1257. Association for Computational Linguistics.

Topic Modeling-based Domain Adaptation for System Combination

Tsuyoshi Okita[1] *Antonio Toral*[1] *Josef van Genabith*[1]
(1) Dublin City University, Glasnevin, Dublin 9
tokita@computing.dcu.ie, atoral@computing.dcu.ie, josef@computing.dcu.ie

ABSTRACT
This paper gives the system description of the domain adaptation team of Dublin City University for our participation in the system combination task in the Second Workshop on Applying Machine Learning Techniques to Optimise the Division of Labour in Hybrid MT (ML4HMT-12). We used the results of unsupervised document classification as meta information to the system combination module. For the Spanish-English data, our strategy achieved 26.33 BLEU points, 0.33 BLEU points absolute improvement over the standard confusion-network-based system combination. This was the best score in terms of BLEU among six participants in ML4HMT-12.

KEYWORDS: Statistical Machine Translation, Topic Model, System Combination.

1 Introduction

This paper describes a new extension to our system combination module developed in Dublin City University (Du and Way, 2010a,b; Okita and van Genabith, 2012). We have added a domain adaptation technique (Foster and Kuhn, 2007; Koehn and Schroeder, 2007; Daumé III, 2007) to our system combination module and tested it in the system combination task at the ML4HMT-2012 workshop.

The study of translation outputs obtained by systems trained on out-of-domain training data has contributed to the advance of domain adaptation techniques for statistical machine translation (SMT) (Foster and Kuhn, 2007; Koehn and Schroeder, 2007; Daumé III, 2007; Pecina et al., 2012). The literature shows that the performance gain obtained by using in-domain data (compared to out-of-domain data) is, in most cases, rather significant. Although it is often the case in the SMT literature that genre classification is done in a supervised setting (Jiang et al., 2012), analogous to genre-specific dictionaries in rule-based machine translation (RBMT) systems, a cache-based approach (Tiedemann, 2010) further investigates this on a fine-grained level of context, which does not need the notion of genre. Therefore, one idea worth exploring is to employ unsupervised document classification to cluster the documents (Blei et al., 2003; Steyvers and Griffiths, 2007; Blei, 2011; Sontag and Roy, 2011; Murphy, 2012).

In the context of system combination, the effect of out-of-domain training data is slightly different. Unlike the training of SMT systems, system combination essentially handles only the translation outputs, which can be considered to be in-domain. However, if we consider a training procedure which takes two steps (Du and Way, 2010a; Okita and van Genabith, 2012), these two steps are possible candidates that have a connection with the out-of-domain data. This two step approach to system combination tunes parameters in the first step over the development set and subsequently produces a final translation combining fragments obtained by translating the test set with different MT systems using such parameters.

Apart from this line of motivation, a number of times we have encountered obstacles to deploy a system combination module whose origin is difficult to trace. Although the system combination strategy works effectively in most cases, with some particular datasets we have experienced difficulties trying to achieve better performance than the single best system. Such cases include the ZH–EN translation task (Ma et al., 2009) and the EN–FR direction in the system combination task at WMT09[1].

In order to investigate this issue, we need to hypothesise what the cause might be. The super confusion network approach of Du and Way (2010a) assumed that the cause was related to the alignment metric. The strategy was then to incorporate not only one alignment metric but multiple metrics. The current paper hypothesises that the genre of the test and tuning sets exhibit variance, hence out-of-domain effects, and that this causes some variance in the performance of each MT system. If this is indeed the case, as is our assumption, the two methods explored in this paper should be effective: to identify and remove the out-of-domain data from the tuning set and to train on in-domain partitioned data.

The remainder of this paper is organized as follows. Section 2 describes our algorithm. In Section 3, our experimental results are presented. We conclude in Section 4.

[1] `http://www.statmt.org/wmt09`

2 Our Algorithm

Our algorithm consists of the following two steps in Algorithm 1.

Algorithm 1 Our Algorithm

Step 1: Run the out-of-domain data cleaning.
Step 2: Run the in-domain data partitioning.

This algorithm applies unsupervised document classification on the source side. The classification results of the source side are naturally linked to the target side since any parallel corpus forms translation pairs. Obviously another possibility would be to apply the unsupervised document classification jointly both of the source and the target sides.

The details of these two steps are explained in the following subsections.

2.1 Unsupervised Document Classification by Topic Model

We used Latent Dirichlet Allocation (LDA) (Blei et al., 2003; Steyvers and Griffiths, 2007; Blei, 2011; Sontag and Roy, 2011; Murphy, 2012) to perform the (unsupervised) classification. LDA represents topics as multinomial distributions over the W unique word-types in the corpus and represents documents as a mixture of topics.

Let C be the number of unique labels in the corpus. Each label c is represented by a W-dimensional multinomial distribution ϕ_c over the vocabulary. For document d, we observe both the words in the document $w^{(d)}$ as well as the document labels $c^{(d)}$. Given the distribution over topics θ_d, the generation of words in the document is captured by the following generative model.

1. For each label $c \in \{1, \ldots C\}$, sample a distribution over word-types $\phi_c \sim$ **Dirichlet**$(\cdot|\beta)$
2. For each document $d \in \{1, \ldots, D\}$
   (a) Sample a distribution over its observed labels $\theta_d \sim$ **Dirichlet**$(\cdot|\alpha)$
   (b) For each word $i \in \{1, \ldots, N_d^W\}$
      i. Sample a label $z_i^{(d)} \sim$ **Multinomial**(θ_d)
      ii. Sample a word $w_i^{(d)} \sim$ **Multinomial**(ϕ_c) from the label $c = z_i^{(d)}$

The LDA model is represented as a graphical model in Figure 1. There are three levels in this figure: the corpus level, the document level and the within document level. The parameters α and β relate to the corpus level, the variables θ_d belong to the document level, and finally the variables z_{dn} and w_{dn} correspond to the word level, which are sampled once for each word in each document.

2.1.1 Out-of-domain Data Cleaning

Using topic modeling (or LDA) as described above, we propose to clean out-of-domain data from the tuning set as follows:

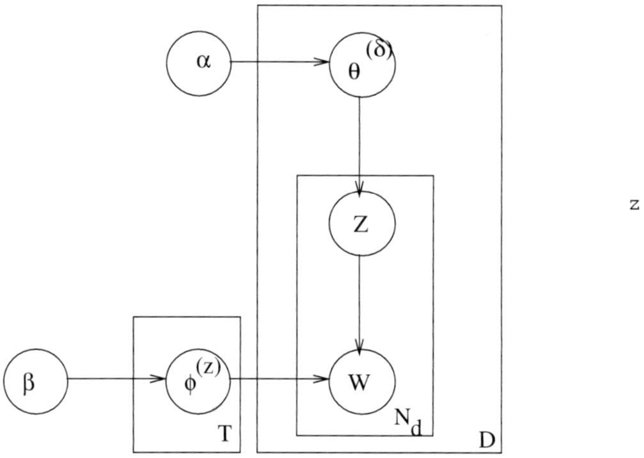

Figure 1: Figure shows the graphical model of LDA.

1. Fix the number of clusters C: choose a relatively big C.[2]

2. Do unsupervised document classification (or LDA) on the source side of the tuning and test sets.

3. Detect the classes that contain only data from the tuning set.

4. Discard the corresponding sentence pairs from the tuning set.

2.1.2 In-domain Data Partitioning

Using topic modeling (or LDA) as described above, we propose to perform in-domain data partitioning as follows:

1. Fix the number of clusters C, we explore values from small to big.[3]

2. Do unsupervised document classification (or LDA) on the source side of the tuning and test sets.

3. Separate each class of tuning and test sets (keep the original index and new index in the allocated separated dataset).

4. Run system combination on each class.

5. Reconstruct the system combined results of each class preserving the original index.

[2] C decides the size of clusters. In our case, 3,003 sentences will be clustered. If $C = 2$, the result cluster size will be 1,500 and we suggest this value of C is slightly too small. If $C = 3,000$, the result cluster size will be 1 and we suggest C is slightly too big. In this case, $C = 500 - 1,000$ would be the range considered and refereed as "relatively big".

[3] Currently, we do not have a definite recommendation on this. It needs to be studied more deeply.

2.2 System Combination

The first step of system combination is to select a backbone by MBR decoding. Let E be the target language, F be the source language, and $M(\cdot)$ be an MT system which maps some sequence in the source language F into some sequence in the target language E. Let $\mathcal{E}$ be the translation outputs of all the participating MT systems. Given a loss function $L(E, E')$ between an automatic translation E' and the reference E, a set of translation outputs $\mathcal{E}$, and an underlying probability model $P(E|F)$, a MBR decoder is defined as in (1) (Kumar and Byrne, 2002):

$$\hat{E} = \arg\min_{E' \in \mathcal{E}} R(E') = \arg\min_{E' \in \mathcal{E}} \sum_{E' \in \mathcal{E}} L(E, E')P(E|F) \tag{1}$$

where $R(E')$ denotes the Bayes risk of candidate translation E' under the loss function L. We use BLEU (Papineni et al., 2002) as this loss function L. According to this selected backbone, other translation outputs are aligned to form a confusion network.

The second step is by the (monotonic) consensus decoding for the given confusion network. There are two cases when this consensus decoding is executed: one is with references (tuning phase) and one is without references (test phase). Let $E_{j,n}$ be the nth best confusion network hypothesis and F_j be the jth source sentence. The hypothesis confidence (Rosti et al., 2007) is given as follows:

$$\log p(E_{j,n}/F_j) = \sum_{i=1}^{N_j-1} \log(\sum_{l=1}^{N_S} \lambda_l p(w|l,i)) + \nu L(E_{j,n}) + \mu N_{nulls}(E_{j,n}) + \xi N_{words}(E_{j,n}) \tag{2}$$

where ν is the language model weight, $L(E_{j,n})$ is the LM log-probability and $N_{words}(E_{j,n})$ is the number of words in the hypothesis $E_{j,n}$. In the tuning phase, the parameters in Equation (2) are tuned. Then, using these tuned parameters, the test phase will be carried out. In this respect, the partitioning of in-domain data is very important. If we partition the in-domain data, the partitioned data will be guaranteed to be in-domain data (if we partition the data in general, the partitioned data will not be guaranteed to be in-domain tuning data).

3 Experimental Results

ML4HMT-2012 provides four translation outputs (*s1* to *s4*) which are MT output by two RBMT systems, APERTIUM and LUCY, PB-SMT (MOSES) and HPB-SMT (MOSES), respectively. The tuning data consists of 20,000 sentence pairs, while the test data consists of 3,003 sentence pairs.

class 1	20000					3003				
class 2	10213	9787				1821	1182			
class 3	6752	6428	6820			838	962	1203		
class 4	4461	4766	5954	4819		785	432	776	1010	
class 5	3846	3669	3665	3978	4842	542	343	1311	404	403

Table 1: Unsupervised document classification by a fixed number of clusters. Each column shows the number of items classified in each class.

Our experimental setting is as follows. We use our system combination module (Du and Way, 2010a,b; Okita and van Genabith, 2012), which has its own language modeling tool, MERT process, and MBR decoding. We use the BLEU metric as loss function in MBR decoding. We

	NIST	BLEU	METEOR	WER	PER
cleaned	7.4945	0.2500	0.5499287	56.6991	42.3032
wo cleaning	7.6846	0.2600	0.5643944	56.2368	41.5399

Table 2: The results of out-of-domain data cleaning compared with without cleaning.

use TERP[4] as alignment metrics in monolingual word alignment.[5] We use MALLET[6] for topic modeling. Although topic modeling is often used to obtain unsupervised clustering, our interest is focused on unsupervised classification of documents.

Given a specified number of classes C, we run MALLET to train the model on the tuning set. In this process, we obtained the label distribution for each document. Then, we infer the class using the trained model which yields the label distribution for each document. Results are shown in Table 1.

	NIST	BLEU	METEOR	WER	PER
s1	6.7456	0.2016	0.5712806	67.2881	54.7614
s2	7.3982	0.2388	0.6195136	63.9684	51.6444
s3	9.4167	0.3400	0.6650655	49.9341	37.4271
s4	9.1167	0.3273	0.6744035	52.0578	38.9179
topic modeling (devset)					
2 class	9.3504	0.3292	0.6529581	50.2061	36.8001
3 class	9.3045	0.3268	0.6522747	50.7730	37.4164
4 class	9.3084	0.3267	0.6513981	50.7391	37.3968
5 class	9.3950	0.3302	0.6531211	50.1131	36.7148
system combination					
syscom	9.2912	0.3268	0.6531500	50.7681	37.2779

Table 3: Table shows the performance of translation outputs s1 to s4 and results of system combination on development set.

Table 2 shows the performance on standard system combination, with and without data cleaning. In this out-of-domain data cleaning, we removed 2,207 sentences (11.0%) from the tuning data. The remaining 17,793 sentences are considered to be in-domain data from the point of view of the test set. However, this out-of-domain data cleaning did not quite work as expected.

Table 3 shows the performance on the development set. The performance of s1 and s2 is radically lower than that of s3 and s4 across all evaluation metrics considered. Although it may be that the performance of s1 and s2 is always inferior to that of the other systems, it may also be that s1 and s2 do not work well for some particular genre (the results shown in Table 4 seem to corroborate this hypothesis, particularly for s2).

We also performed the in-domain partitioning with the out-of-domain tuning set and without using the out-of-domain tuning set. Table 4 shows our results when we partitioned into 2, 3, 4, and 5 clusters.

The results show that 4 class classification achieved the best result, namely 26.33 BLEU points.

[4] `http://www.cs.umd.edu/~snover/terp`

[5] For example, Du and Way (2010a) explains various monolingual alignment methods such as TER alignment, HMM alignment and IHMM alignment.

[6] `http://mallet.cs.umass.edu/`

This is an improvement of 0.33 BLEU points absolute over system combination without topic modeling. Note that the baseline achieved 26.00 BLEU points, the best single system in terms of BLEU was s4 which achieved 25.31 BLEU points, and the best single system in terms of METEOR was s2 which achieved 0.5853.

	NIST	BLEU	METEOR	WER	PER
s1	6.4996	0.2248	0.5458641	64.2452	49.9806
s2	6.9281	0.2500	0.5853446	62.9194	48.0065
s3	7.4022	0.2446	0.5544660	58.0752	44.0221
s4	7.2100	0.2531	0.5596933	59.3930	44.5230
topic modeling (testset)					
2 class	7.7036	0.2620	0.5626187	55.8092	41.7783
3 class	7.7134	0.2628	0.5645200	55.8865	41.7171
4 class	7.7146	0.2633	0.5647685	55.8612	41.7264
5 class	7.6245	0.2592	0.5620755	56.9575	42.6229
system combination without topic modeling					
syscom	7.6846	0.2600	0.5643944	56.2368	41.5399

Table 4: Table includes our results on testset (the row 4 to 7).

Conclusion and Perspectives

This paper deployed domain adaptation via unsupervised document clustering through topic modeling and applied it to system combination. On the one hand, the out-of-domain data cleaning lost 1 BLEU point compared to the results of standard system combination. On the other hand, the in-domain data partitioning improved 1.02 BLEU points absolute compared to the single best MT system, and improved 0.33 BLEU points absolute compared to the results of the standard system combination approach.

Further studies will be carried out to explore this topic. First, this paper only handled the partition size of at most 5. We would like to apply our method to a larger dataset. It is also interesting to seek a method to find the optimal number of clusters automatically by hierarchical clustering methods with non-parametric Baysian methods (Okita and Way, 2010, 2011a,b). Alternatively, we have an interest on the reason why the out-of-domain data cleaning did not work in connection with noise if there is a link (Okita, 2009; Okita et al., 2010a,b; Okita, 2012).

Second, although we described only the method that uses domain adaptation, we explored also the correction of the output based on corresponding tokens and PoS tags from the source and target sides (e.g. if a token in the source side is a singular noun and the corresponding target token is a plural noun, overwrite that token by its singular form). This is related to techniques we have explored for diagnostic evaluation using checkpoints (Naskar et al., 2011; Toral et al., 2012) and a more detailed study is necessary to apply them in system combination.

Acknowledgments

This research is partly supported by the 7th Framework Programme and the ICT Policy Support Programme of the European Commission through the T4ME (Grant agreement No. 249119) and the PANACEA (contract no. 248064) projects as well as by Science Foundation Ireland (Grant No. 07/CE/I1142) as part of the Centre for Next Generation Localisation (www.cngl.ie) at Dublin City University.

References

Blei, D., Ng, A. Y., and Jordan, M. I. (2003). Latent Dirichlet allocation. *Journal of Machine Learning Research*, 3:993–1022.

Blei, D. M. (2011). Introduction to probabilistic topic models. *Communications of the ACM.*

Daumé III, H. (2007). Frustratingly easy domain adaptation. In *Conference of the Association for Computational Linguistics (ACL)*, Prague, Czech Republic.

Du, J. and Way, A. (2010a). An incremental three-pass system combination framework by combining multiple hypothesis alignment methods. *International Journal of Asian Language Processing*, 20(1):1–15.

Du, J. and Way, A. (2010b). Using TERp to augment the system combination for SMT. *In Proceedings of the Ninth Conference of the Association for Machine Translation (AMTA2010).*

Foster, G. and Kuhn, R. (2007). Mixture-model adaptation for SMT. *In Proceedings of the Second ACL Workshop on Statistical Machine Translation*, page 128–135.

Jiang, J., Way, A., Ng, N., Haque, R., Dillinger, M., and Lu, J. (2012). Monolingual data optimisation for bootstrapping SMT engines. *In the Proceedings of the MONOMT-2012 Workshop at AMTA.*

Koehn, P. and Schroeder, J. (2007). Experiments in domain adaptation for Statistical Machine Translation. *In Proceedings of the ACL Workshop on Statistical Machine Translation.*

Kumar, S. and Byrne, W. (2002). Minimum Bayes-Risk word alignment of bilingual texts. *In Proceedings of the Empirical Methods in Natural Language Processing (EMNLP 2002)*, pages 140–147.

Ma, Y., Okita, T., Cetinoglu, O., Du, J., and Way, A. (2009). Low-resource Machine Translation using MaTrEx: the DCU Machine Translation system for IWSLT 2009. *In Proceedings of the International Workshop on Spoken Language Translation (IWSLT 2009)*, pages 29–36.

Murphy, K. P. (2012). Machine learning: A probabilistic perspective. *The MIT Press.*

Naskar, S. K., Toral, A., Gaspari, F., and Way, A. (2011). A framework for diagnostic evaluation of MT based on linguistic checkpoints. *In the Proceedings of the Machine Translation Summit XIII*, pages 529–536.

Okita, T. (2009). Data cleaning for word alignment. *In Proceedings of Joint Conference of the 47th Annual Meeting of the Association for Computational Linguistics and the 4th International Joint Conference on Natural Language Processing of the Asian Federation of Natural Language Processing (ACL-IJCNLP 2009) Student Research Workshop*, pages 72–80.

Okita, T. (2012). Annotated corpora for word alignment between Japanese and English and its evaluation w ith MAP-based word aligner. In Calzolari, N., Choukri, K., Declerck, T., Doğan, M. U., Maegaard, B., Mariani, J., Odijk, J., and Piperidis, S., editors, *Proceedings of the Eighth International Conference on Language Resources and Evalu ation (LREC-2012)*, pages 3241–3248, Istanbul, Turkey. European Language Resources Association (ELRA). ACL Anthology Identifier: L12-1655.

Okita, T., Graham, Y., and Way, A. (2010a). Gap between theory and practice: Noise sensitive word alignment in Machine Translation. *In Proceedings of the Workshop on Applications of Pattern Analysis (WAPA2010). Cumberland Lodge, England.*

Okita, T., Guerra, A. M., Graham, Y., and Way, A. (2010b). Multi-Word Expression sensitive word alignment. *In Proceedings of the Fourth International Workshop On Cross Lingual Information Access (CLIA2010, collocated with COLING2010), Beijing, China.*, pages 1–8.

Okita, T. and van Genabith, J. (2012). Minimum Bayes risk decoding with enlarged hypothesis space in system combination. *In Proceedings of the 13th International Conference on Intelligent Text Processing and Computational Linguistics (CICLING 2012). LNCS 7182 Part II. A. Gelbukh (Ed.)*, pages 40–51.

Okita, T. and Way, A. (2010). Hierarchical Pitman-Yor Language Model in Machine Translation. *In Proceedings of the International Conference on Asian Language Processing (IALP 2010).*

Okita, T. and Way, A. (2011a). Given bilingual terminology in Statistical Machine Translation: MWE-sensitve word alignment and hierarchical Pitman-Yor process-based translation model smoothing. *In Proceedings of the 24th International Florida Artificial Intelligence Research Society Conference (FLAIRS-24)*, pages 269–274.

Okita, T. and Way, A. (2011b). Pitman-Yor process-based language model for Machine Translation. *International Journal on Asian Language Processing*, 21(2):57–70.

Papineni, K., Roukos, S., Ward, T., and Zhu, W. (2002). BLEU: a method for automatic evaluation of machine translation. In *ACL*, pages 311–318.

Pecina, P., Toral, A., Papavassiliou, V., Prokopidis, P., and van Genabith, J. (2012). Domain adaptation of Statistical Machine Translation using web-crawled resources: a case study. In *EAMT 2012: Proceedings of the 16th Annual Conference of the European Association for Machine Translation*, pages 145–152, Trento, Italy.

Rosti, A.-V. I., Matsoukas, S., and Schwartz, R. (2007). Improved word-level system combination for Machine Translation. *In Proceedings of the 45th Annual Meeting of the Association for Computational Linguistics*, pages 312–319.

Sontag, D. and Roy, D. M. (2011). The complexity of inference in Latent Dirichlet Allocation. *In Advances in Neural Information Processing Systems 24 (NIPS).*

Steyvers, M. and Griffiths, T. (2007). Probabilistic topic models. *Handbook of Latent Semantic Analysis. Psychology Press.*

Tiedemann, J. (2010). Context adaptation in Statistical Machine Translation using models with exponentially decaying cache. *In Proceedings of the ACL Workshop on Domain Adaptation for Natural Language Processing.*

Toral, A., Naskar, S. K., Gaspari, F., and Groves, D. (2012). DELiC4MT: A Tool for Diagnostic MT Evaluation over User-defined Linguistic Phenomena. *The Prague Bulletin of Mathematical Linguistics*, pages 121–132.

Sentence-Level Quality Estimation for MT System Combination

Tsuyoshi Okita[1] *Raphaël Rubino*[2] *Josef van Genabith*[3]
(1) Dublin City University, Glasnevin, Dublin 9
(2) NCLT, Dublin City University, Glasnevin, Dublin 9
(3) CNGL, Dublin City University, Glasnevin, Dublin 9
tokita@computing.dcu.ie,
raphael.rubino@computing.dcu.ie,josef@computing.dcu.ie

ABSTRACT
This paper provides the system description of the Dublin City University system combination module for our participation in the system combination task in the Second Workshop on Applying Machine Learning Techniques to Optimize the Division of Labour in Hybrid MT (ML4HMT-12). We incorporated a sentence-level quality score, obtained by sentence-level Quality Estimation (QE), as meta information guiding system combination. Instead of using BLEU or (minimum average) TER, we select a backbone for the confusion network using the estimated quality score. For the Spanish-English data, our strategy improved 0.89 BLEU points absolute compared to the best single score and 0.20 BLEU points absolute compared to the standard system combination strategy.

KEYWORDS: Statistical Machine Translation, System Combination, Quality Estimation.

1 Introduction

This paper describes a new extension to our system combination module in Dublin City University. We deployed a Quality Estimation technique (Blatz et al., 2003; Rubino et al., 2012) in our system combination module for the system combination task in the ML4HMT-2012 workshop.

System combination is a strategy (Bangalore et al., 2001; Matusov et al., 2006; Tromble et al., 2008; Du and Way, 2010; DeNero et al., 2009; Okita and van Genabith, 2012) that provides a way to combine multiple translation outputs from potentially very different MT systems including Rule-based MT (RBMT) and SMT. It is often the case that a practical system combination strategy involves a confusion network (Matusov et al., 2006), which is also the case in our system, in order to combine fragments from a number of systems. The standard process to build such confusion networks consists of two steps: (1) a selection of a backbone (or a skeleton), and (2) monolingual word alignment (Matusov et al., 2006; Sim et al., 2007; He et al., 2008; Karakos et al., 2008) between a backbone and other hypotheses in a pairwise manner. Once such a confusion network is built, we can search for the best path using a (monotonic) consensus network decoder. It is noted that there are also approaches which select multiple possible hypotheses as backbones (Leusch and Ney, 2010).

One important factor in the overall performance of such a system combination method resides in the selection of a backbone, which is the main focus in this paper. There are several reasons why a good backbone selection is very important. First, in practice, it is often the case that the final translation output is identical to the backbone even if the overall combination method includes a confusion network. Second, it depends on the backbone whether some segments which do not match with the backbone will be discarded. In fact, important segments potentially contributing to good translation quality, may not be considered only because such fragments do not match with the backbone.

Rosti et al. (2007) propose (minimum average) TER to select a backbone. This alignment metric selects the hypotheses that agrees with the other hypotheses on average. Another common alignment metric is BLEU (Tromble et al., 2008; Du and Way, 2010; Duh et al., 2011; Okita and van Genabith, 2012). This metric selects a hypothesis that performs best. This paper proposes a novel method to use (sentence-level) Quality Estimation (QE) to select a backbone. Since QE quantifies the confidence of the MT output (Specia et al., 2009), this selection would roughly in line with BLEU, which selects the best performing hypothesis as a backbone. Note that one difference is that BLEU and TER are used as a loss function in MBR decoding (Kumar and Byrne, 2002; Sim et al., 2007), while we select the best sentence in terms of (sentence-level) QE. Hence, in doing so, we do not minimize the worst case risk.

The main part of this paper provides an algorithm to use QE as the selection mechanism of a backbone of a confusion network. However, such a selection, by itself, can be considered as one method of (sentence-level) system combination. What is more, the two QE-based methods yield translation outputs which differ in quality. Because of this, this paper presents two algorithms: (1) system combination via QE-selected backbone, and (2) QE-based sentence selection.

The remainder of this paper is organized as follows. Section 2 describes our algorithms. In Section 3, our experimental results are presented. We conclude in Section 3.2.

2 Our Method

We describe the QE-based backbone selection method used in our algorithm in Subsection 2.1. Following this, we briefly outline how we used QE as (sentence-level) system combination (the 2nd algorithm of this paper). Subsection 2.2 incorporates this QE method to select a backbone.

2.1 Sentence-Level QE

QE methods (Blatz et al., 2003) are developed for situations where references are not available, which contrasts with automatic MT evaluation using BLEU (Papineni et al., 2002) and TER (Snover et al., 2006). The approach described in this subsection is based on QE at the sentence level. To select one translation from the four systems participating in our system combination approach, we want to predict quality scores for all the translations and pick the translation with the best score. To obtain these scores, we first use the tuning dataset and compute TER scores at the sentence level for each translation output of the four systems individually. These scores, associated with feature vectors corresponding to the source and target sentence pairs, are used to train a regression model. This model is then used to predict *TER* scores on the test dataset.

2.1.1 Experimental Setup

The machine learning toolkit used in our experiments is LibSVM (Chang and Lin, 2011), an implementation of the Support Vector Regression (SVR) method. We use the Radial Basis Function (RBF) kernel as it is widely used in the QE for the MT community and it usually achieves good performance (Specia et al., 2009; Soricut et al., 2012). An important aspect of SVR with RBF kernel is hyper parameter optimization. In our setup, three parameters have to be optimized: c (the penalty factor), γ (the kernel parameter) and ϵ (the approximated function accuracy level).

$$MAE = \frac{1}{n}\sum_{i=1}^{n}|ref_i - pred_i| \quad (1) \qquad RMSE = \sqrt{\frac{1}{n}\sum_{i=1}^{n}(ref_i - pred_i)^2} \quad (2)$$

We optimize these parameters using *grid-search*, an iterative process computing n-fold cross-validation on each possible triplet of parameters and selecting the best set of parameters according to a score (usually the Mean Absolute Error or the Root Mean Square Error, described in 1 and 2, where n is the number of test instances, ref and $pred$ are the reference and predicted TER scores of the ith test instance respectively). This method is expensive in terms of computing time (we use 5-fold cross-validation at each iteration) and it is not feasible do do this in an acceptable amount of time for the whole tuning set provided by the shared task (20k sentences pairs for each MT system). To tackle this issue, we extract a reduced development set from the tuning set using the cosine distance to measure the proximity between the test and the tuning feature vectors. For each MT system, we iterate over the corresponding test feature vectors and measure the cosine distance with all the feature vectors of the tuning set. We keep the tuning instances which are most similar to the test instances to build our reduced development set. This set is used to optimize the three hyper parameters of ϵ-SVR. Finally, four regression models are built (one for each MT system) using the complete tuning set and the optimized parameters.

2.1.2 Feature Sets

In order to capture relevant information from the source sentences and their translations, we extract different types of features which capture information about the source sentence complexity, the target sentence fluency, but also the difference between the four MT systems' outputs.

Surface – These features are extracted directly by analyzing the source and the target sentences. 10 features are extracted from the source and the target sentences: sentence length, average word length, number of punctuation marks, number of upper-case letters and average number of words in the sentence. 5 features are given by the source and target ratio of the previous features. A total of 15 features are extracted from the surface information.

Language Model – A total of 6 LM features are extracted from the source and the target sentences according to 5-gram Kneser-Ney discounted LMs built using the SRILM toolkit (Stolcke, 2002) (2 log-probability scores, 4 perplexity scores with or without start and end of sequence tags).

MT Outputs Difference – To capture the difference between the four MT outputs given one source sentence, we consider iteratively each MT output as a *translation reference* and compare it to the three other MT outputs using the software TERCOM[1]. This method allows us to extract detailed information about the number of insertions, deletions, substitutions, etc., as well as the TER scores between the current MT output and the others. A total of 30 features are extracted following this procedure.

From these three feature sources, we build two feature sets. The first feature set, corresponding to our first revision (**R1**), contains only target LM features and the MT Output Difference features, with a total of 33 features. The LM used to extract the features is built using the target side of the tuning set provided by the shared task organizers. The second feature set, corresponding to our second revision (**R2**), contains all the features presented in this section, with a total of 51 features. The LMs used to extract the features are built using EUROPARL[2], JRC-ACQUIS[3], and UN CORPUS[4] whose size is around 160,000k sentence pairs.

2.2 System Combination

The first step is to select a backbone using the results of QE method described in the last Subsection 2.1. In the second step, based on the backbone selected in the first step, we build the confusion network by aligning the hypotheses with the backbone. In this process, we used the TER distance (Snover et al., 2006) between the backbone and the hypotheses. We do this for all the hypotheses sentence by sentence. Note that in this process, deleted words are substituted as NULL words (or ϵ-arcs).

In the third step, the consensus translation is extracted as the best path in the confusion network. This (monotonic) consensus decoding selects the best word $\hat{e}_k$ by the word posterior probability via voting at each position k in the confusion network, as in (3):

$$\hat{E}_k = \arg\max_{e \in \mathcal{E}} p_k(e|F) \tag{3}$$

[1]http://www.cs.umd.edu/~snover/tercom/tercom-0.7.25.tgz
[2]http://www.statmt.org/europarl
[3]http://ipsc.jrc.ec.europa/
[4]http://www.statmt.org/wmt12/translation-task.html

but with the following features as well: 4-gram and 5-gram target language model, word length penalty, and NULL word length penalty. Note that Minimum Error-Rate Training (MERT) is used to tune the weights of the confusion network.

3 Experiments

ML4HMT-2012 provides four translation outputs *s1* to *s4* from APERTIUM, LUCY, PB-SMT (MOSES) and HPB-SMT (MOSES). The tuning data consists of 20,000 sentence pairs while the test data consists of 3,003 sentence pairs.

Our experimental setting is as follows. We use our system combination module (Du and Way, 2010; Okita and van Genabith, 2012) which includes a language modeling tool, a MERT process, and MBR decoding of its own. We use the BLEU metric as loss function in MBR decoding. We use TERP[5] as alignment metrics in monolingual word alignment.

3.1 Pre-study: Evaluation of QE Model

We evaluated our QE model on the test set by predicting TER scores at the sentence level and comparing them with the reference. We used two measures described by the equations 1 and 2. The scores are presented in Table 1. These results were quite surprising because the larger feature set (**R2**) did not reach the best results in terms of TER score prediction. Using only target LM features based on a small dataset and the MT output differences (**R1**) leads to MAE scores between 0.21 and 0.17. For this feature set, the most accurate sentence level score prediction was obtained on the MT system *s3*, which corresponds to the PBSMT implementation MOSES, while the system *s2*, which corresponds to the RBMT system LUCY, leads to the worse score prediction. In other words, it is more difficult to predict sentence-level scores of *s2* compared to *s3*.

	s1		s2		s3		s4	
	MAE	RMSE	MAE	RMSE	MAE	RMSE	MAE	RMSE
R1	0.19	0.26	0.21	0.29	0.17	0.24	0.18	0.25
R2	0.20	0.26	0.21	0.29	0.21	0.28	0.20	0.26

Table 1: Error scores of the QE model when predicting TER scores at the sentence level on the test set for the four MT systems.

3.2 Main Results

Table 2 shows the performance on the development set. Table 3 shows the results of Algorithm 1 and 2. The first four lines show the single best performance of each translation output where s4 achieves 25.31 BLEU points which is the best among four MT systems. The standard system combination results, shown in the next line, was 26.00 BLEU points, which improved 0.69 BLEU points absolute. We used two different feature set in the QE method: R1 corresponds to the small feature set, while R2 corresponds to the larger feature set.

Results for the first algorithm (system combination with QE) are shown in the next two lines. R1 achieved 26.20 BLEU points, which improved 0.89 BLEU points absolute compared to the best single system. R1 improved 0.20 BLEU points absolute compared to the standard

[5] `http://www.cs.umd.edu/~snover/terp`

	NIST	BLEU	METEOR	WER	PER
s1	6.7456	0.2016	0.5712806	67.2881	54.7614
s2	7.3982	0.2388	0.6195136	63.9684	51.6444
s3	9.4167	0.3400	0.6650655	49.9341	37.4271
s4	9.1167	0.3273	0.6744035	52.0578	38.9179
System combination without QE (standard)					
syscom	9.2912	0.3268	0.6531500	50.7681	37.2779

Table 2: Table shows the performance of translation outputs s1 to s4 and results of system combination on development set.

system combination results. R2 achieved 26.00 BLEU points, which improved 0.69 BLEU points absolute, which did not improve over the standard system combination results.

	NIST	BLEU	METEOR	WER	PER
s1	6.4996	0.2248	0.5458641	64.2452	49.9806
s2	6.9281	0.2500	0.5853446	62.9194	48.0065
s3	7.4022	0.2446	0.5544660	58.0752	44.0221
s4	7.2100	0.2531	0.5596933	59.3930	44.5230
System combination without QE (standard)					
sys	7.6846	0.2600	0.5643944	56.2368	41.5399
System combination with QE (1st algorithm)					
R1	7.6846	0.2620	0.5642806	56.0051	41.5226
R2	7.5076	0.2600	0.5661256	58.2736	43.1051
System combination with QE (s2,s3,s4)					
R1	7.5273	0.2523	0.5556744	57.6502	43.5260
R2	7.5318	0.2528	0.5561100	57.7168	43.4528
Backbone Performance (2nd Algorithm)					
R1	7.4654	0.2501	0.5536140	57.6795	43.3782
R2	7.4777	0.2530	0.5581949	57.7634	43.2809

Table 3: This table includes our results by 1st algorithm and 2nd algorithm.

Conclusion and perspectives

This paper presents the method to use QE for backbone selection in system combination. This strategy improved 0.89 BLEU points absolute compared to the best single system and 0.20 BLEU points absolute compared to the standard system combination strategy.

However, there are two issues. At first sight, our strategy seemed to work quite well as explained in Section 3. Table 4 shows results using two other ways to select a backbone. The

	NIST	BLEU	METEOR	WER	PER
min ave TER	7.6231	0.2638	0.5652795	56.3967	41.6092
s2 backbone	7.6371	0.2648	0.5606801	56.0077	42.0075

Table 4: This table shows the performance when the backbone was selected by average TER and by one of the good backbone.

first method used the minimum average TER (Rosti et al., 2007) while the second method simply selects the output of system 2 (Lucy LT RBMT system outputs). The second method is based on the intuition that the output of Lucy LT RBMT system is more likely to be grammatically well-formed compared to the other MT outputs. This is somewhat surprising but this result was the best among the methods.

Table 5 shows two examples where TER scores at the sentence-level are used to compare the QE and the system combination outputs. In Case A, the QE output has a higher TER score compared to that of the system combination, while it is the opposite in Case B. We observe in both cases that the QE output leads to a better translation adequacy, even when its TER score is lower than the system combination output. This is related to the features based on the target LM (log-probability and perplexities) used in our QE approach. In Case B particularly, the system combination leads to a better TER score but the negation "no" is replaced by "do", which leads to a lower adequacy. These two cases emphasize the fact that a better automatic score does not necessarily means a better translation quality.

	System Combination TER Degradation (Case A)
src	*"Me voy a tener que apuntar a un curso de idiomas", bromea.*
QE	'I am going to have to point to a language course "joke.
comb	I am going to have to point to a of course ", kids.
ref	"I'll have to get myself a language course," he quips.
	System Combination TER Improvement (Case B)
src	*Sorprendentemente, se ha comprobado que los nuevos concejales casi no comprenden esos conocidos conceptos.*
QE	Surprisingly, it appears that the new councillors almost no known understand these concepts.
comb	Surprisingly, it appears that the new councillors almost do known understand these concepts.
ref	Surprisingly, it turned out that the new council members do not understand the well-known concepts.

Table 5: Translation output comparison between the standalone Quality Estimation approach and the System Combination.

Further study is, thus, required to investigate these two issues. Especially regarding the first issue, we would like to examine the rationale behind why the backbone provided by Lucy RBMT achieves the highest score even though this system is not the best performing system, neither in terms of BLEU nor TER, but provides translation output which is more grammatical than the other MT outputs.

Additionally, it is also possible that the reason why our method did perform less than Lucy backbone may be related to the performance of monolingual word alignment. If this is the case, the monolingual version of MAP-based word aligner which can incorporate prior knowledge (Okita et al., 2010b,a; Okita and Way, 2011; Okita, 2012) may be the next target.

Acknowledgments

This research is partly supported by the 7th Framework Programme and the ICT Policy Support Programme of the European Commission through the T4ME project (Grant agreement No. 249119) as well as by Science Foundation Ireland (Grant No. 07/CE/I1142) as part of the Centre for Next Generation Localisation (www.cngl.ie) at Dublin City University.

References

Bangalore, S., Bordel, G., and Riccardi, G. (2001). Computing consensus translation from multiple Machine Translation systems. *In Proceedings of the IEEE Automatic Speech Recognition and Understanding Workshop (ASRU)*, pages 350–354.

Blatz, J., Fitzgerald, E., Foster, G., Gandrabur, S., Goutte, C., Kulesza, A., Sanchis, A., and Ueffing, N. (2003). Confidence Estimation for Machine Translation. In *JHU/CLSP Summer Workshop Final Report*.

Chang, C.-C. and Lin, C.-J. (2011). LIBSVM: A library for Support Vector Machines. *ACM Transactions on Intelligent Systems and Technology*, 2:27:1–27:27.

DeNero, J., Chiang, D., and Knight, K. (2009). Fast consensus decoding over translation forests. *In proceedings of the Joint Conference of the 47th Annual Meeting of the ACL and the 4th International Joint Conference on Natural Language Processing of the AFNLP*, pages 567–575.

Du, J. and Way, A. (2010). An incremental three-pass system combination framework by combining multiple hypothesis alignment methods. *International Journal of Asian Language Processing*, 20(1):1–15.

Duh, K., Sudoh, K., Wu, X., Tsukada, H., and Nagata, M. (2011). Generalized minimum Bayes risk system combination. In *Proceedings of 5th International Joint Conference on Natural Language Processing*, pages 1356–1360, Chiang Mai, Thailand. Asian Federation of Natural Language Processing.

He, X., Yang, M., Gao, J., Nguyen, P., and Moore, R. (2008). Indirect-HMM-based hypothesis alignment for combining outputs from Machine Translation systems. *In Proceedings of Empirical Methods in Natural Language Processing (EMNLP08)*, page 98–107.

Karakos, D., Eisner, J., Khudanpur, S., and Dreyer, M. (2008). Machine Translation system combination using ITG-based alignments. *In Proceedings of the 46th Annual Meeting of the Association for Computational Linguistics (ACL-08)*, page 81–84.

Kumar, S. and Byrne, W. (2002). Minimum Bayes-Risk word alignment of bilingual texts. *In Proceedings of the Empirical Methods in Natural Language Processing (EMNLP 2002)*, pages 140–147.

Leusch, G. and Ney, H. (2010). The RWTH system combination system for WMT 2010. *In Proceedings of the Joint 5th Workshop on Statistical Machine Translation and MetricsMATR*, pages 315–320.

Matusov, E., Ueffing, N., and Ney, H. (2006). Computing consensus translation from multiple Machine Translation systems using enhanced hypotheses alignment. *In Proceedings of the 11st Conference of the European Chapter of the Association for Computational Linguistics (EACL)*, pages 33–40.

Okita, T. (2012). Annotated Corpora for Word Alignment between Japanese and English and its Evaluation with MAP-based Word Aligner. In Calzolari, N., Choukri, K., Declerck, T., Doğan, M. U., Maegaard, B., Mariani, J., Odijk, J., and Piperidis, S., editors, *Proceedings of the Eighth International Conference on Language Resources and Evaluation (LREC-2012)*, pages 3241–3248, Istanbul, Turkey. European Language Resources Association (ELRA). ACL Anthology Identifier: L12-1655.

Okita, T., Graham, Y., and Way, A. (2010a). Gap Between Theory and Practice: Noise Sensitive Word Alignment in Machine Translation. *In Proceedings of the Workshop on Applications of Pattern Analysis (WAPA2010). Cumberland Lodge, England.*

Okita, T., Guerra, A. M., Graham, Y., and Way, A. (2010b). Multi-Word Expression sensitive word alignment. *In Proceedings of the Fourth International Workshop On Cross Lingual Information Access (CLIA2010, collocated with COLING2010), Beijing, China.*, pages 1–8.

Okita, T. and van Genabith, J. (2012). Minimum Bayes risk decoding with enlarged hypothesis space in system combination. *In Proceedings of the 13th International Conference on Intelligent Text Processing and Computational Linguistics (CICLING 2012). LNCS 7182 Part II. A. Gelbukh (Ed.)*, pages 40–51.

Okita, T. and Way, A. (2011). Given Bilingual Terminology in Statistical Machine Translation: MWE-sensitve Word Alignment and Hierarchical Pitman-Yor Process-based Translation Model Smoothing. *In Proceedings of the 24th International Florida Artificial Intelligence Research Society Conference (FLAIRS-24)*, pages 269–274.

Papineni, K., Roukos, S., Ward, T., and Zhu, W. (2002). BLEU: a method for automatic evaluation of Machine Translation. In *ACL*, pages 311–318.

Rosti, A.-V. I., Matsoukas, S., and Schwartz, R. (2007). Improved Word-Level System Combination for Machine Translation. *In Proceedings of the 45th Annual Meeting of the Association for Computational Linguistics*, pages 312–319.

Rubino, R., Foster, J., Wagner, J., Roturier, J., Kaljahi, R. S. Z., and Hollowood, F. (2012). DCU-Symantec submission for the WMT 2012 quality estimation task. *In Proceedings of WMT*.

Sim, K. C., Byrne, W. J., Gales, M. J., Sahbi, H., and Woodland, P. C. (2007). Consensus network decoding for Statistical Machine Translation system combination. *In Proceedings of the ICASSP*, 4:105–108.

Snover, M., Dorr, B., Schwartz, R., Micciulla, L., and Makhoul, J. (2006). A study of Translation Edit Rate with targeted human annotation. In *Proceedings of Association for Machine Translation in the Americas*, pages 223–231.

Soricut, R., Bach, N., and Wang, Z. (2012). The SDL language weaver systems in the WMT12 quality estimation shared task. In *Proceedings of the Seventh Workshop on Statistical Machine Translation*, pages 145–151, Montréal, Canada. Association for Computational Linguistics.

Specia, L., Cancedda, N., Dymetman, M., Turchi, M., and Cristianini, N. (2009). Estimating the sentence-level quality of Machine Translation systems. In *EAMT*, pages 28–35.

Stolcke, A. (2002). SRILM-an extensible language modeling toolkit. In *InterSpeech*, volume 2, pages 901–904.

Tromble, R., Kumar, S., Och, F., and Macherey, W. (2008). Lattice minimum Bayes-risk decoding for Statistical Machine Translation. *Proceedings of the 2008 Conference on Empirical Methods in Natural Language Processing*, pages 620–629.

Neural Probabilistic Language Model for System Combination

Tsuyoshi Okita[1]
(1) Dublin City University, Glasnevin, Dublin 9
tokita@computing.dcu.ie

ABSTRACT
This paper gives the system description of the neural probabilistic language modeling (NPLM) team of Dublin City University for our participation in the system combination task in the Second Workshop on Applying Machine Learning Techniques to Optimise the Division of Labour in Hybrid MT (ML4HMT-12). We used the information obtained by NPLM as meta information to the system combination module. For the Spanish-English data, our paraphrasing approach achieved 25.81 BLEU points, which lost 0.19 BLEU points absolute compared to the standard confusion network-based system combination. We note that our current usage of NPLM is very limited due to the difficulty in combining NPLM and system combination.

KEYWORDS: statistical machine translation, neural probabilistic language model, system combination.

1 Introduction

This paper describes a new extension to our system combination module developed in Dublin City University (Du and Way, 2010a,b; Okita and van Genabith, 2012). We have added a neural probabilistic language model (NPLM) (Bengio et al., 2000, 2005) to our system combination module and tested it in the system combination task at the ML4HMT-2012 workshop.

A neural probabilistic language model (NPLM) (Bengio et al., 2000, 2005) and the distributed representations (Hinton et al., 1986) provide an idea to achieve the better perplexity than n-gram language model (Stolcke, 2002) and their smoothed language models (Kneser and Ney, 1995; Chen and Goodman, 1998; Teh, 2006). Recently, the latter one, i.e. smoothed language model, has had a lot of developments in the line of nonparametric Bayesian methods such as hierarchical Pitman-Yor language model (HPYLM) (Teh, 2006) and Sequence Memoizer (SM) (Wood et al., 2009; Gasthaus et al., 2010), including an application to SMT (Okita and Way, 2010a,b, 2011). A NPLM considers the representation of data in order to make the probability distribution of word sequences more compact where we focus on the similar semantical and syntactical roles of words. For example, when we have two sentences *"The cat is walking in the bedroom"* and *"A dog was running in a room"*, these sentences can be more compactly stored than the n-gram language model if we focus on the similarity between (the, a), (bedroom, room), (is, was), and (running, walking). Thus, a NPLM provides the semantical and syntactical roles of words as a language model. A NPLM of Bengio et al. (2000) implemented this using the multi-layer neural network and yielded 20% to 35% better perplexity than the language model with the modified Kneser-Ney methods (Chen and Goodman, 1998).

There are several successful applications of NPLM (Schwenk, 2007; Collobert and Weston, 2008; Schwenk, 2010; Collobert, 2011; Collobert et al., 2011; Deschacht et al., 2012; Schwenk et al., 2012). First, one category of applications include POS tagging, NER tagging, and parsing (Collobert et al., 2011; Bordes et al., 2011). This category uses the features provided by a NPLM in the limited window size.[1] It is often the case that there is no such long range effects that the decision cannot be made beyond the limited windows which requires to look carefully the elements in a long distance. Second, the other category of applications include Semantic Role Labeling (SRL) task (Collobert et al., 2011; Deschacht et al., 2012). This category uses the features within a sentence. A typical element is the predicate in a SRL task which requires the information which sometimes in a long distance but within a sentence. Both of these approaches do not require to obtain the best tag sequence, but these tags are independent. Third, the final category includes MERT process (Schwenk, 2010) and possibly many others where most of them remain undeveloped. The objective of this learning in this category is not to search the best tag for a word but the best sequence for a sentence. Hence, we need to apply the sequential learning approach.[2] Although most of the applications described in (Collobert and Weston, 2008; Collobert, 2011; Collobert et al., 2011; Deschacht et al., 2012) are monolingual tasks, the application of this approach to a bilingual task introduces really astonishing aspects, which we can call "creative words" (Veale, 2012), automatically into the traditional resource constrained SMT components. For example, the training corpus of word aligner is often strictly restricted to the

[1]It is possible to implement a parser in the way of the second category. However, we adopt the categorization which was implemented by (Collobert et al., 2011).

[2]The first and second approaches do not often appear in the context of SMT, while the third category includes most of the decoding algorithm appeared in SMT including MAP decoding, MBR decoding, and (monotonic) consensus decoding. The latter two decoding appears in system combination.

given parallel corpus. However, a NPLM allows this training with huge monolingual corpus. Although most of this line has not been even tested mostly due to the problem of computational complexity of training NPLM, Schwenk et al. (2012) applied this to MERT process which reranks the n-best lists using NPLM. This paper aims at different task, a task of system combination (Bangalore et al., 2001; Matusov et al., 2006; Tromble et al., 2008; Du et al., 2009; DeNero et al., 2009; Okita and van Genabith, 2012). This category of tasks employs the sequential method such as Maximum A Posteriori (MAP) inference (Viterbi decoding) (Koller and Friedman, 2009; Sontag, 2010; Murphy, 2012) on Conditional Random Fields (CRFs) / Markov Random Fields (MRFs). [3]

The remainder of this paper is organized as follows. Section 2 describes our algorithms. In Section 3, our experimental results are presented. We conclude in Section 4.

2 Our Algorithms

The aim of NPLM is to capture the semantically and syntactically similar words in a way that a latent word depends on the context. There would be many ways to use this language model. However, one difficulty resides in how such information can be incorporated to the module of system combination. Due to this difficulty, we present here a method which is rather restricted despite the power of NPLM.

This paper presents two methods based on the intuitive observation that we will get the variety of words if we condition on the fixed context, which would form paraphrases in theory. Then, we present the second method that we examine the dependency structure of candidates sentence replaced with alternative expressions (or paraphrases). Our algorithms consist of three steps shown in Algorithm 1. The details of Step 1 and 2 will be explained in Section 2.1 and Step 3 will be explained in Section 2.2.

Algorithm 1 Our Algorithm

Given: For given testset g, prepare N translation outputs $\{s_1, \ldots, s_N\}$ from several systems.
Step 1: Train NPLM with monolingual corpus. Note that this monolingual corpus would be better in the same domain as the testset g.
Step 2: Modify the translation outputs $\{s_1, \ldots, s_N\}$ replaced with alternative expressions (or paraphrases).
Step 3: Augment the sentences of translation outputs prepared in Step 2.
Step 4: Run the system combination module.

2.1 Paraphrasing using NPLM

2.1.1 Plain Paraphrasing

We introduce our algorithm via a word sense disambiguation (WSD) task which selects the right disambiguated sense for the word in question. This task is necessary due to the fact that a text is natively ambiguous accommodating with several different meanings. The task of WSD (Deschacht et al., 2012) can be written as in (1):

$$P(\text{synset}_i | \text{features}_i, \theta) = \frac{1}{Z(\text{features})} \prod_m g(\text{synset}_i, k)^{f(\text{feature}_i^k)} \quad (1)$$

[3]Note that the (monotonic) consensus decoding in system combination is the subset of this.

where k ranges over all possible features, $f(\text{feature}_i^k)$ is an indicator function whose value is 1 if the feature exists, and 0 otherwise, $g(\text{synset}_i, k)$ is a parameter for a given synset and feature, θ is a collection of all these parameters in $g(\text{synset}_i, k)$, and Z is a normalization constant. Note that we use the term "synset" as an analogy of the WordNet (Miller, 1995): this is equivalent to "sense" or "meaning". Note also that NPLM will be included as one of the features in this equation. If features include sufficient statistics, a task of WSD will succeed. Otherwise, it will fail.

Now we assume that the above WSD component was trained. We would like to consider the paraphrasing in connection with this. We consider a sentence with some words replaced by the alternative surface form. In this context, we are interested in the words which share the same synset (or meaning) but the realized surface form is different. Let us denote $P(\text{surface}_i|\text{synset}_j, \text{features}_k, \theta)$ by the probability of such words. Then, we suppose that we compare P(surface$_i$=x_i | synset$_j$,features$_k$,θ) and P(surface$_i$=x_i' | synset$_j$,features$_k$,θ) under the condition that synset$_j$, features$_k$, and θ are the same, and that the relationships below hold as in (2):

$$P(\text{surface}_i = x_i|\text{synset}_j, \text{features}_k, \theta) > P(\text{surface}_i = x_i'|\text{synset}_j, \text{features}_k, \theta) \quad (2)$$

Then, the alternative surfaces form x_i in higher probability will be chosen instead of the other one x_i' among paraphrases $\{x_i, x_i'\}$ of this word.

On the one hand, the paraphrases obtained in this way have attractive aspects that can be called "a creative word" (Veale, 2012). This is since the traditional resource that can be used when building a translation model by SMT are constrained on paralell corpus. However, NPLM can be trained on huge monolingual corpus. On the other hand, unfortunately in practice, the notorious training time of NPLM only allows us to use fairly small monolingual corpus although many papers made an effort to reduce it (Mnih and Teh, 2012). Due to this, we cannot ignore the fact that NPLM trained not on a huge corpus may be affected by noise. Conversely, we have no guarantee that such noise will be reduced if we train NPLM on a huge corpus. It is quite likely that NPLM has a lot of noise for small corpora. Hence, this paper also needs to provide the way to overcome difficulties of noisy data. In order to avoid this difficulty, we limit the paraphrase only when it includes itself in high probability.

2.1.2 Paraphrasing with Modified Dependency Score

Although we modified a suggested paraphrase without any intervention in the above algorithm, it is also possible to examine whether such suggestion should be adopted or not. If we add paraphrases and the resulted sentence has a higher score in terms of the modified dependency score (Owczarzak et al., 2007) (See Figure 1), this means that the addition of paraphrases is a good choice. If the resulted score decreases, we do not need to add them. One difficulty in this approach is that we do not have a reference which allows us to score it in the usual manner. For this reason, we adopt the *naive way* to deploy the above and we deploy this with *pseudo references*. First, if we add paraphrases and the resulted sentence does not have a very bad score, we add these paraphrases since these paraphrase are not very bad (*naive* way). Second, we do scoring between the sentence in question with *all the other candidates* (*pseudo references*) and calculate an average of them. Thus, our second algorithm is to select a paraphrase which may not achieve a very bad score in terms of the modified dependency score using NPLM.

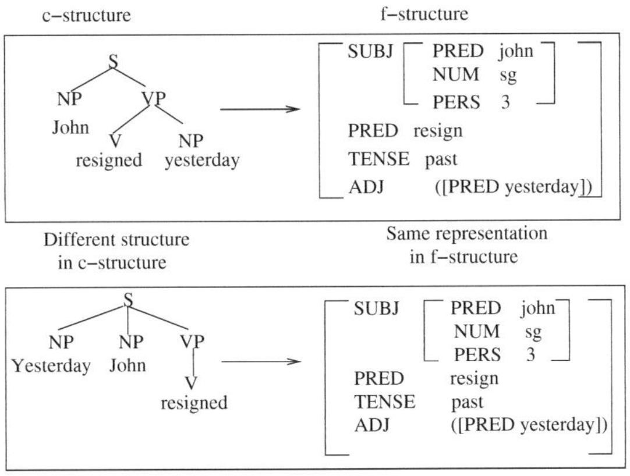

Figure 1: By the modified dependency score (Owczarzak et al., 2007), the score of these two sentences, "John resigned yesterday" and "Yesterday John resigned", are the same. Figure shows c-structure and f-structure of two sentences using Lexical Functional Grammar (LFG) (Bresnan, 2001).

Modified Dependency Score We mention here the reason why we use the modified dependency score. First, unlike BLEU or NIST, the modified dependency score can capture the syntactical construction and grammaticality of sentences. Second, our current dataset seems to be interesting since it includes Lucy LT RBMT outputs. (The last year's ML4HMT-11 (Okita and van Genabith, 2011) also included the translation output of Lucy LT RBMT outputs.) If we choose the entire Lucy's output as a backbone and run a system combination, the resulted score is the highest among various system combination strategies we tried (See "s2 backbone" in Table 2). These two facts suggest us the following strategy: if we have prior knowledge that the Lucy backbone will obtain a high score, it would be interesting to start from the Lucy backbone and pursue whether we can improve the overall score further by adding paraphrases. As is evident from the fact that the Lucy backbone is good, our interest will not be BLEU or NIST, but MODIFIED DEPENDENCY SCORE. This may lead to a higher BLEU score than the system combination results with Lucy backbone. Note that in order to make it a universal algorithm, we need to remove Lucy backbone from this algorithm. Hence, only the modified dependency score remains, which forms the algorithm already mentioned.

system	translation output	precision	recall	F-score
s1	these do usually in a week .	0.080	0.154	0.105
s2	these are normally made in a week .	0.200	0.263	0.227
s3	they are normally in one week .	0.080	0.154	0.105
s4	they are normally on a week .	0.120	0.231	0.158
ref	the funding is usually offered over a one-week period .			

Table 1: An example of modified dependency score for a set of translation outputs.

2.2 System Combination

As is mentioned at the beginning of this section, the interface between the NPLM and system combination has some difficulties. This contrasts with the task of n-best reranking

(Schwenk et al., 2012). In the case of n-best reranking, the probability provided by NPLM can be used immediately in the re-evaluation of the n-best lists.

Difficulties of Interface In our case, due to the reason below despite the advantage of word varieties it is difficult to incorporate this into the translation outputs in a straight forward way. The two decoding strategies used by a confusion network-based system combination, i.e. MBR decoding and (monotonic) consensus decoding, have difficulties in each step.

First, in MBR decoding in the first step, the inputs, i.e. each translation outputs, are quantified by the loss function with its score in the sentence level. This mechanism does not allow us to add fragments freely in the word level. Therefore, it requires us to increase the number of sentences with only a slight replacement in the sentence level. This paper takes this strategy for the first step to circumvent this difficulty.

Second, in (monotonic) consensus decoding in the second step, the word posterior probabilities in the confusion network do not reflect the probability quantified globally, but is rather locally in accordance with other probability of words in the same position. Similarly, one way would be to augment in the sentence level.

Inputs to System Combination Module We check the possibilities whether the word can have alternative expression and whether the probability of such expression is bigger than that of the original word or not. If this holds, we replace such words with alternative expressions. This will make a new sentence.

3 Experimental Results

ML4HMT-2012 provides four translation outputs (*s1* to *s4*) which are MT outputs by two RBMT systems, APERTIUM and LUCY, PB-SMT (MOSES) and HPB-SMT (MOSES), respectively. The tuning data consists of 20,000 sentence pairs, while the test data consists of 3,003 sentence pairs.

Our experimental setting is as follows. We use our system combination module (Du and Way, 2010a,b; Okita and van Genabith, 2012), which has its own language modeling tool, MERT process, and MBR decoding. We use the BLEU metric as loss function in MBR decoding. We use TERP[4] as alignment metrics in monolingual word alignment. We trained NPLM using 500,000 sentence pairs from English side of EN-ES corpus of EUROPARL[5].

(a)	*the Government wants to limit the torture of the " witches " , as it published in a brochure*
(b)	the Government wants to limit the torture of the " witches " , as it published in the proceedings
(a)	*the women that he " return " witches are sent to an area isolated , so that they do not hamper the rest of the people .*
(b)	the women that he " return " witches are sent to an area eligible , so that they do not affect the rest of the country .

Table 2: Table includes two examples of plain paraphrase.

The results show that the first algorithm of NPLM-based paraphrased augmentation, that is

[4] `http://www.cs.umd.edu/~snover/terp`
[5] `http://www.statmt.org/europarl`

NPLM plain, achieved 25.61 BLEU points, which lost 0.39 BLEU points absolute over the standard system combination. The second algorithm, NPLM dep, achieved slightly better results of 25.81 BLEU points, which lost 0.19 BLEU points absolute over the standard system combination. Note that the baseline achieved 26.00 BLEU points, the best single system in terms of BLEU was s4 which achieved 25.31 BLEU points, and the best single system in terms of METEOR was s2 which achieved 0.5853.

	NIST	BLEU	METEOR	WER	PER
s1	6.4996	0.2248	0.5458641	64.2452	49.9806
s2	6.9281	0.2500	0.5853446	62.9194	48.0065
s3	7.4022	0.2446	0.5544660	58.0752	44.0221
s4	7.2100	0.2531	0.5596933	59.3930	44.5230
NPLM plain	7.6041	0.2561	0.5593901	56.4620	41.8076
NPLM dep	7.6213	0.2581	0.5601121	56.1334	41.7820
BLEU-MBR	7.6846	0.2600	0.5643944	56.2368	41.5399
min ave TER-MBR	7.6231	0.2638	0.5652795	56.3967	41.6092
DA	7.7146	0.2633	0.5647685	55.8612	41.7264
QE	7.6846	0.2620	0.5642806	56.0051	41.5226
s2 backbone	7.6371	0.2648	0.5606801	56.0077	42.0075
modDep precision	7.6670	0.2636	0.5659757	56.4393	41.4986
modDep recall	7.6695	0.2642	0.5664320	56.5059	41.5013
modDep Fscore	7.6695	0.2642	0.5664320	56.5059	41.5013

	modDep precision	modDep recall	modDep Fscore
average s1	0.244 (586)	0.208	0.225
average s2	0.250 (710)	0.188	0.217
average s3	0.189 (704)	0.145	0.165
average s4	0.195 (674)	0.167	0.180

Table 3: This table shows single best performance, the performance of two algorithms in this paper (NPLM plain and dep), MBR-decoding with BLEU loss function and TER loss function, the performance of domain adaptation (Okita et al., 2012b) and quality estimation (Okita et al., 2012a), the performance of Lucy backbone, and the performance of the selection of sentences by modified dependency score (precision, recall, and F-score each). The four lines at the bottom marked with average s1 to s4 indicates the average performance of s1 in terms of precision, recall, and F-score (from the 2nd to 4th columns) when we make the backbone by choosing the maximum score in terms of the modified dependency score. For example, the first line of "modDep precision" shows when we chose a backbone by the maximum modified dependency score in terms of precision. 586 sentences were selected from s1, 710 sentences were from s2, and so forth. The average BLEU score of these 586 sentences was 24.4.

Conclusion and Perspectives

This paper deployed meta information obtained by NPLM into a system combination module. NPLM captures the semantically and syntactically similar words in a way that a latent word depends on the context. First, we interpret the information obtained by NPLM as paraphrases with regard to the translation outputs. Then, we incorporate the augmented sentences as inputs to the system combination module. Unfortunately, this strategy lost 0.39 BLEU points absolute compared to the standard confusion network-based system combination. A revised strategy to assess the quality of paraphrases achieved 25.81 BLEU points, which lost 0.19 BLEU points absolute.

There are many further avenues. First, as already mentioned, this paper only scratched the surface of NPLM. One problem was the interface between NPLM and system combination. Our motivation behind using NPLM was the possibility that NPLM would supply the semantically and syntactically rich synonyms and similar words to the rather restricted translation outputs, as well as the traditional functions as LM, which are to be supplied to the system combination module. For this reason, we believe that paraphrases generated using NPLM will not be a bad direction. However, there would be other approach as well. Collobert and Weston (2008) and Bordes et al. (2011) integrate NPLM in their software. When we integrate our approach, one way would be to implement it without employing the knowledge of paraphrases. It would be interesting to compare this and our approaches in this paper. Alternatively, prior knowledge about the speriority of Lucy output can be embedded into system combination by prior (Okita et al., 2010b,a; Okita, 2012).

Second, we show some positive results about the modified dependency score (Owczarzak et al., 2007). We used this as sentence-based criteria to select a backbone in three ways: maximum precision, recall, and F-score. Results are shown in Table 3. Indeed, these criteria worked quite well. Unfortunately, these scores were still lower than that of Lucy's backbone. The lower parts of this table show statistics when we select a backbone by the modified dependency score. Interestingly, the modified dependency score of s2 (Lucy) was the best in precision score, but was not the best in recall or in F-score. This shows that the selection of backbone by the modified dependency score did not work as much as that of the (fixed) Lucy backbone. We need to search another explanation why the Lucy backbone obtained the highest score.

Third, this paper did not mention much about noise. Understanding the mechanism of noise on NPLM may be related to the learning mechanism of NPLM, if we draw an analogy from the case when we examined the noise of word alignment (Okita, 2009; Okita et al., 2010b). This may also be related to the smoothing mechanism (Okita and Way, 2010a,b, 2011).

Acknowledgments

We thank Maite Melero for proof-reading. This research is partly supported by the 7th Framework Programme and the ICT Policy Support Programme of the European Commission through the T4ME (Grant agreement No. 249119) project as well as by Science Foundation Ireland (Grant No. 07/CE/I1142) as part of the Centre for Next Generation Localisation (www.cngl.ie) at Dublin City University.

References

Bangalore, S., Bordel, G., and Riccardi, G. (2001). Computing consensus translation from multiple machine translation systems. *In Proceedings of the IEEE Automatic Speech Recognition and Understanding Workshop (ASRU)*, pages 350–354.

Bengio, Y., Ducharme, R., and Vincent, P. (2000). A neural probabilistic language model. *In Proceedings of Neural Information Systems.*

Bengio, Y., Schwenk, H., Senécal, J.-S., Morin, F., and Gauvain, J.-L. (2005). Neural probabilistic language models. *Innovations in Machine Learning: Theory and Applications Edited by D. Holmes and L. C. Jain.*

Bordes, A., Glorot, X., Weston, J., and Bengio, Y. (2011). Towards open-text semantic parsing via multi-task learning of structured embeddings. *CoRR*, abs/1107.3663.

Bresnan, J. (2001). Lexical functional syntax. *Blackwell*.

Chen, S. and Goodman, J. (1998). An empirical study of smoothing techniques for language modeling. *Technical report TR-10-98 Harvard University*.

Collobert, R. (2011). Deep learning for efficient discriminative parsing. *In Proceedings of the 14th International Conference on Artificial Intelligence and Statistics (AISTATS)*.

Collobert, R. and Weston, J. (2008). A unified architecture for natural language processing: Deep neural networks with multitask learning. *In International Conference on Machine Learning (ICML 2008)*.

Collobert, R., Weston, J., Bottou, L., Karlen, M., Kavukcuoglu, K., and Kuksa, P. (2011). Natural language processing (almost) from scratch. *Journal of Machine Learning Research*, 12:2493–2537.

DeNero, J., Chiang, D., and Knight, K. (2009). Fast consensus decoding over translation forests. *In proceedings of the Joint Conference of the 47th Annual Meeting of the ACL and the 4th International Joint Conference on Natural Language Processing of the AFNLP*, pages 567–575.

Deschacht, K., Belder, J. D., and Moens, M.-F. (2012). The latent words language model. *Computer Speech and Language*, 26:384–409.

Du, J., He, Y., Penkale, S., and Way, A. (2009). MaTrEx: the DCU MT System for WMT 2009. *In Proceedings of the Third EACL Workshop on Statistical Machine Translation*, pages 95–99.

Du, J. and Way, A. (2010a). An incremental three-pass system combination framework by combining multiple hypothesis alignment methods. *International Journal of Asian Language Processing*, 20(1):1–15.

Du, J. and Way, A. (2010b). Using terp to augment the system combination for smt. *In Proceedings of the Ninth Conference of the Association for Machine Translation (AMTA2010)*.

Gasthaus, J., Wood, F., and Teh, Y. W. (2010). Lossless compression based on the sequence memoizer. *DCC 2010*.

Hinton, G. E., McClelland, J. L., and Rumelhart, D. (1986). Distributed representations. *Parallel Distributed Processing: Explorations in the Microstructure of Cognition(Edited by D.E. Rumelhart and J.L. McClelland) MIT Press*, 1.

Kneser, R. and Ney, H. (1995). Improved backing-off for n-gram language modeling. *In Proceedings of the IEEE International Conference on Acoustics, Speech and Signal Processing*, pages 181–184.

Koller, D. and Friedman, N. (2009). Probabilistic graphical models: Principles and techniques. *MIT Press*.

Matusov, E., Ueffing, N., and Ney, H. (2006). Computing consensus translation from multiple machine translation systems using enhanced hypotheses alignment. *In Proceedings of the 11st Conference of the European Chapter of the Association for Computational Linguistics (EACL)*, pages 33–40.

Miller, G. A. (1995). Wordnet: A lexical database for english. *Communications of the ACM*, 38(11):39–41.

Mnih, A. and Teh, Y. W. (2012). A fast and simple algorithm for training neural probabilistic language models. In *Proceedings of the International Conference on Machine Learning*.

Murphy, K. P. (2012). Machine learning: A probabilistic perspective. *The MIT Press*.

Okita, T. (2009). Data cleaning for word alignment. *In Proceedings of Joint Conference of the 47th Annual Meeting of the Association for Computational Linguistics and the 4th International Joint Conference on Natural Language Processing of the Asian Federation of Natural Language Processing (ACL-IJCNLP 2009) Student Research Workshop*, pages 72–80.

Okita, T. (2012). Annotated corpora for word alignment between japanese and english and its evaluation w ith map-based word aligner. In Calzolari, N., Choukri, K., Declerck, T., Doğan, M. U., Maegaard, B., Mariani, J., Odijk, J., and Piperidis, S., editors, *Proceedings of the Eighth International Conference on Language Resources and Evalu ation (LREC-2012)*, pages 3241–3248, Istanbul, Turkey. European Language Resources Association (ELRA). ACL Anthology Identifier: L12-1655.

Okita, T., Graham, Y., and Way, A. (2010a). Gap between theory and practice: Noise sensitive word alignment in machine translation. *In Proceedings of the Workshop on Applications of Pattern Analysis (WAPA2010). Cumberland Lodge, England.*

Okita, T., Guerra, A. M., Graham, Y., and Way, A. (2010b). Multi-Word Expression sensitive word alignment. *In Proceedings of the Fourth International Workshop On Cross Lingual Information Access (CLIA2010, collocated with COLING2010), Beijing, China.*, pages 1–8.

Okita, T., Rubino, R., and van Genabith, J. (2012a). Sentence-level quality estimation for mt system combination. *In Proceedings of ML4HMT Workshop (collocated with COLING 2012)*.

Okita, T., Toral, A., and van Genabith, J. (2012b). Topic modeling-based domain adaptation for system combination. *In Proceedings of ML4HMT Workshop (collocated with COLING 2012)*.

Okita, T. and van Genabith, J. (2011). DCU Confusion Network-based System Combination for ML4HMT. *Shared Task on Applying Machine Learning techniques to optimising the division of labour in Hybrid MT (ML4HMT-2011, collocated with LIHMT-2011)*.

Okita, T. and van Genabith, J. (2012). Minimum bayes risk decoding with enlarged hypothesis space in system combination. *In Proceedings of the 13th International Conference on Intelligent Text Processing and Computational Linguistics (CICLING 2012). LNCS 7182 Part II. A. Gelbukh (Ed.)*, pages 40–51.

Okita, T. and Way, A. (2010a). Hierarchical pitman-yor language model in machine translation. *In Proceedings of the International Conference on Asian Language Processing (IALP 2010)*.

Okita, T. and Way, A. (2010b). Pitman-Yor process-based language model for Machine Translation. *International Journal on Asian Language Processing*, 21(2):57–70.

Okita, T. and Way, A. (2011). Given bilingual terminology in statistical machine translation: Mwe-sensitve word alignment and hierarchical pitman-yor process-based translation model smoothing. *In Proceedings of the 24th International Florida Artificial Intelligence Research Society Conference (FLAIRS-24)*, pages 269–274.

Owczarzak, K., van Genabith, J., and Way, A. (2007). Evaluating machine translation with LFG dependencies. *Machine Translation*, 21(2):95–119.

Schwenk, H. (2007). Continuous space language models. *Computer Speech and Language*, 21:492–518.

Schwenk, H. (2010). Continuous space language models for statistical machine translation. *The Prague Bulletin of Mathematical Linguistics*, 83:137–146.

Schwenk, H., Rousseau, A., and Attik, M. (2012). Large, pruned or continuous space language models on a gpu for statistical machine translation. *In Proceeding of the NAACL workshop on the Future of Language Modeling*.

Sontag, D. (2010). Approximate inference in graphical models using LP relaxations. *Massachusetts Institute of Technology (Ph.D. thesis)*.

Stolcke, A. (2002). SRILM – An extensible language modeling toolkit. *In Proceedings of the International Conference on Spoken Language Processing*, pages 901–904.

Teh, Y. W. (2006). A hierarchical bayesian language model based on pitman-yor processes. *In Proceedings of the 44th Annual Meeting of the Association for Computational Linguistics (ACL-06), Prague, Czech Republic*, pages 985–992.

Tromble, R., Kumar, S., Och, F., and Macherey, W. (2008). Lattice minimum bayes-risk decoding for statistical machine translation. *Proceedings of the 2008 Conference on Empirical Methods in Natural Language Processing*, pages 620–629.

Veale, T. (2012). Exploding the creativity myth: The computational foundations of linguistic creativity. *London: Bloomsbury Academic*.

Wood, F., Archambeau, C., Gasthaus, J., James, L., and Teh, Y. W. (2009). A stochastic memoizer for sequence data. *In Proceedings of the 26th International Conference on Machine Learning*, pages 1129–1136.

System Combination Using Joint, Binarised Feature Vectors

Christian FEDERMANN[1]
(1) DFKI GmbH, Language Technology Lab,
Stuhlsatzenhausweg 3, D-66123 Saarbrücken, GERMANY
cfedermann@dfki.de

Abstract
We describe a method for system combination based on joint, binarised feature vectors. Our method can be used to combine several black-box source systems. We first define a total order on given translation output which can be used to partition an n-best list of translations into a set of pairwise system comparisons. Using this data, we explain how an SVM-based classification model can be trained and how this classifier can be applied to combine translation output on the sentence level. We describe our experiments for the ML4HMT-12 shared task and conclude by giving a summary of our findings and by discussing future extensions and experiments using the proposed approach.

Keywords: Machine Translation, System Combination, Machine Learning.

1 Introduction

Research efforts on machine translation (MT) have resulted in many different methods and MT paradigms, each having individual strengths and weaknesses. There exist approaches following linguistic theory as well as data-driven methods relying on statistical processing with only little linguistic knowledge involved. In recent years, there has also been a lot of research on the automatic combination of machine translation output, resulting in so-called hybrid MT engines.

Regardless of the actual method implemented in a given machine translation system, creating translation output usually requires several, often heterogeneous, features. These can be 1) simple scores, e.g., for language model scores, parser or phrase table probabilities; 2) more complex data such as hierarchical parse trees or word alignment links; or 3) even full parse forests or n-best lists.

Given this wide range of heterogenous features and their diversity, it is very difficult to get an *intuitive* understanding of the inner workings of the MT engine in question; thus, further research work on the combination of machine translation systems into better, hybrid MT systems seems to be of high importance to the field. To overcome the aforementioned problem of incomprehensible feature values, we propose a method based on Machine Learning (ML) tools, leaving the exact interpretation and weighting of features to the ML algorithms.

The remainder of this paper is structured in the following way. After having set the topic in this section, we briefly describe relevant related work in Section 2 before defining and explaining our Machine-Learning-based hybrid MT framework in Section 3. We first give an overview on the basic approach in Subsection 3.1 and then discuss the two most important components: the order on translations is defined in Subsection 3.2 while the notion of joint, binarised feature vectors for ML is introduced in Subsection 3.3. We discuss the experiments conducted for the ML4HMT-12 shared task in Section 4 and then conclude by giving a summary of our findings and by discussing upcoming research in Section 5.

2 Related Work

Hybrid machine translation methods and system combination approaches have been receiving a lot of research attention over the last decade. Several papers, including seminal work from (Frederking and Nirenburg, 1994), support the general belief that it is possible to combine translation output from different systems achieving an improvement over the individual baseline systems.

System combination on the phrasal level can be realised using so-called *Confusion Networks*. Previous work on this approach are described in more detail in (Federmann et al., 2009; Federmann and Hunsicker, 2011). The algorithm chooses one of the given MT systems as *backbone* or *skeleton* of the hybrid translation, while all other translations are connected using word alignment techniques. Together, the systems then form a network with different paths through the network resulting in different translations.

Next to phrasal combination methods, there also are approaches that focus on preserving the syntactic structure of the translation backbone, and hence perform *Sentence-based Combination*. Here, several given black-box translations are re-scored or re-ranked in order to determine the best translation for a given sentence in the source text. This is similar to *Re-ranking Approaches* in SMT. See related work from (Avramidis, 2011), (Gamon et al., 2005), or (Rosti et al., 2007).

Finally, there are *Machine-Learning-based Combination* approaches which train classifiers to assess the quality of given translation output. Recent work (He et al., 2010) applies such Machine Learning tools to estimate translation quality and re-rank a set of translations on the sentence level.

3 Methodology

3.1 Classification-Based Hybrid MT

In this Section, we describe our architecture for hybrid machine translation. It is based on classifiers trained using state-of-the-art Machine-Learning tools. Given a set of n translations from several systems that are treated as "black boxes" and a development set including corresponding reference, we perform the following processing steps to generate a hybrid translation for some given test set:

1. Compute a total order of individual system output on the development set using some order relation based on quality assessment of the translations with automatic metrics. This can also be defined to include results from, e.g., manual evaluation;
2. Decompose the aforementioned system ranking into a set of pairwise comparisons for any two pairs of systems A, B. As we do not allow for ties in our system comparisons, the two possible values $A > B, A < B$ also represent our *Machine-Learning classes* $+1/-1$, respectively;
3. Annotate the translations with feature values derived from NLP tools such as *language models*, *part-of-speech taggers*, or *parsers*;
4. Create a data set for training an SVM-based classifier that can estimate which of two given systems A, B is *better* according to the available features;
5. Train an SVM-based classifier model using, e.g., `libSVM`, see (Chang and Lin, 2011);

Steps 1–5 represent the *training phase* in our framework. The availability of a development set including references is required as this is needed to allow the definition of an ordering relation which subsequently defines the training instances for the SVM-based classifier. After training, we can use the classifier as follows:

6. Apply the resulting classification onto the candidate translations from the given test set. This will produce pairwise estimates $+1/-1$ for each possible pair of systems A, B;
7. Perform *round-robin system elimination* to determine the single best system from the set of candidate translations on a per sentence level;
8. Using this data, synthesise the final, hybrid translation output.

Steps $6-8$ represent the *decoding phase* in which the trained classifier is applied to a set of *unseen* translations without any reference text available. By computing pairwise *winners* for each possible pair of systems and each individual sentence of the test set, we determine the single best system on the sentence level. The methodology is explained in more detail in (Federmann, 2012b,c).

3.2 A Total Order on Translations

In order to rank the given source translations, we first need to define an *ordering relation* over the set of translation outputs. For this, we consider manual judgements wherever available and, as a fallback, also apply three renowned evaluation metrics which are the *de-facto standards* for automated assessment of machine translation quality:

1. The Meteor score, on the sentence and on the corpus level, see (Denkowski and Lavie, 2011);
2. The NIST n-gram cooccurence score on the corpus level, see (Doddington, 2002); and
3. The BLEU score which is the most widely used evaluation metric, see (Papineni et al., 2002).

While both the BLEU and the NIST scores are designed to have a high correlation with judgements from manual evaluation on the corpus level, the Meteor metric can also be used to meaningfully compare translation output on the level of individual sentences. We make use of this property when defining our order $ord(A,B)$ on translations, as described in (Federmann, 2012c).

3.3 Using Joint, Binarised Feature Vectors

Many Machine-Learning-based approaches for system combination use classifiers to estimate the quality of or *confidence* in an individual translation output and compare it to other translations afterwards. This means that the feature vector for a given translation A is computed solely on information available from features of A, not considering any other translation B as additional source of information, or formally:

$$vec_{single}(A) \stackrel{\text{def}}{=} \begin{pmatrix} f_1(A) \\ \vdots \\ f_n(A) \end{pmatrix} \in \mathbb{R}^n \tag{1}$$

We aim to explicitly model *pairwise feature comparisons* of translations A, B, storing *binary values* to model if a given feature value $f_x(A)$ for system A is better or worse than corresponding feature value $f_x(B)$ for the competing system B. Effectively, this means that, in our approach, we compare translations *directly* when constructing the set of training instances. Equation 2 shows the formal definition of a so-called *joint, binarised* feature vector:

$$vec_{binarised}(A,B) \stackrel{\text{def}}{=} \begin{pmatrix} f_1(A) > f_1(B) \\ \vdots \\ f_n(A) > f_n(B) \end{pmatrix} \in \mathbb{B}^n \tag{2}$$

The reason to store binary features values $f_x \in \mathbb{B}$ lies in the fact that these can be processed more efficiently during SVM training. Also, previous experiments (Federmann, 2012a; Hunsicker et al., 2012) have shown that the usage of actual feature values $f_x \in \mathbb{R}$ in the feature vector does not give any additional benefit so that we decided to switch to binary notation instead[1]. Note that the order in which features for translations A, B are compared does not strictly matter. For the sake of consistency, we have decided to compare feature values using simple $A > B$ operations, leaving the actual interpretation of these values or their polarity to the Machine Learning toolkit.

3.4 Creating Translations Using a Classifier

Given an SVM classifier trained on joint, binary feature vectors as previously described, we can now create hybrid translation output. A schematic overview is depicted in Figure 1. We compute the best translation for each sentence in the test set, based on the $+1/-1$ output of the classifier for a total of $\frac{n(n-1)}{2}$ unique comparisons.

For each sentence, we create a lookup table that stores for some system X the set of systems which were outperformed by X according to our classifier. To do so, we consider each pairwise comparison of systems A, B and, for each of these, compute the corresponding feature vector which is then

[1] Also note that by using, e.g., *combined feature vectors*, which are comprised of feature values $f_{1-n}(A)$ followed by features $f_{1-n}(B)$, the amount of training data required for meaningful training of a machine learning classifier would need to be increased.

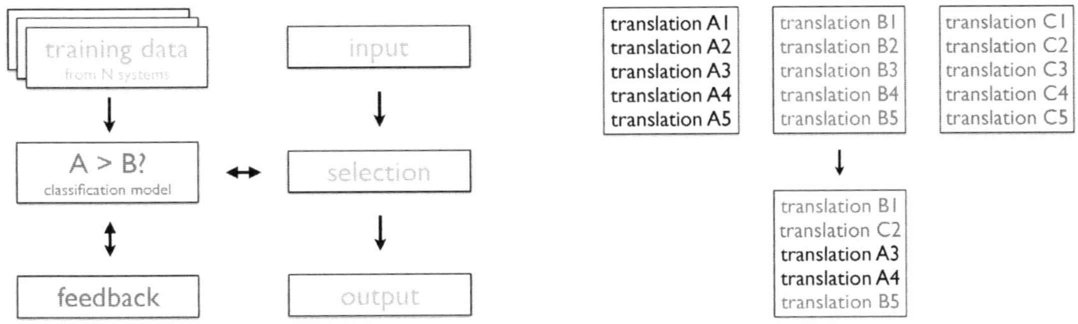

Figure 1: Schematic overview illustrating how an SVM classifier can be used to determine the single best translation using round robin playoff elimination. This operates on the sentence level.

classified by the SVM classifier. Only systems winning at least once during these comparisons end up as keys in our table. The cardinality of the resulting set of outperformed systems implicitly represents the number of wins for a system X. There are three cases to consider:

1. There is exactly one top-ranked system which becomes the translation for the current sentence;
2. Two systems are top-ranked, so the decision depends on the comparison of these. As we do not allow for ties in our comparisons, this is guaranteed to determine a single winner;
3. If more than two systems are top-ranked, we check if one of the systems outperforms the others. In rare cases, this may not yield a winner and we have to fall back to a pre-defined winner, usually the best system from training.

4 Experiments

We worked on a submission for language pair Spanish→English. For this language pair, translation output from four different translation engines was made available by the organisers of the shared task. For each of the systems both translation output and system-specific annotations could be used. As our method relies on *comparable features*, we decided to extract features for all candidate systems ourselves, hence constraining ourselves to only using the given translation output.

We created the data set for classifier training using the following selection of linguistic features:

- number of target tokens, parse tree nodes, and parse tree depth;
- ratio of target/source tokens, parse tree nodes, and parse tree depth;
- n-gram score for n-gram order $n \in \{1, \ldots, 5\}$;
- perplexity for n-gram order $n \in \{1, \ldots, 5\}$.

These features represent a combination of (shallow) parsing and language model scoring and are derived from the set of features that are most often used in the Machine-Learning-based system combination literature.

We use the Stanford Parser (Klein and Manning, 2003) to process the source text and the corresponding translations. For language model scoring, we use the SRILM toolkit (Stolcke, 2002) training a 5-gram language model for English. In this work, we do not consider any source language models.

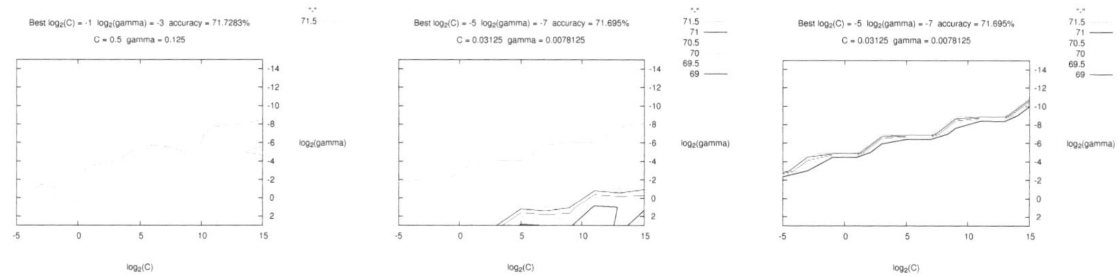

Figure 2: Optimisation grids for linear (left), polynomial (middle), and sigmoid (right) kernels. Note how the decision boundary of the optimal area manifests itself from left to right.

Figure 2 shows the optimisation grids for linear (left), polynomial (middle), and sigmoid (right) kernels. Note how the decision boundary of the optimal area manifests itself from left to right. We ended up using a sigmoid kernel ($C = 2$, $\gamma = 0.015625$) and observed a prediction rate of 68.9608% on the training instances.

5 Conclusion

We have described our submission to the ML4HMT-12 shared task which is based on a Machine-Learning-based framework for hybrid Machine Translation. Using so-called joint, binarised feature vectors, we implemented an algorithm that applies an SVM-based classifier to generate hybrid translations for the language pair Spanish→English. Combination is done on the sentence level.

Upcoming work will involve the refinement of our set of linguistic features and subsequent training and tuning of a Machine Learning classifier to improve the proposed method on additional data. We have already achieved promising baseline results in this respect and look forward to further test our approach, e.g., for ML4HMT-12's second language pair Chinese→English.

The total order on translation output described in Section 3 can be altered to also consider results from manual judgements regarding translation quality. This has not yet been used for our submission, but it would be an interesting extension of this paper.

Acknowledgments

This work has been supported by the Seventh Framework Programme for Research and Technological Development of the European Commission through the T4ME contract (grant agreement: 249119).

References

Avramidis, E. (2011). DFKI System Combination with Sentence Ranking at ML4HMT-2011. In *Proceedings of the International Workshop on Applying Machine Learning Techniques to Optimise the Division of Labour in Hybrid Machine Translation (ML4HMT)*, Barcelona, Spain. META-NET.

Chang, C.-C. and Lin, C.-J. (2011). LIBSVM: A Library for Support Vector Machines. *ACM Transactions on Intelligent Systems and Technology*, 2:27:1–27:27.

Denkowski, M. and Lavie, A. (2011). Meteor 1.3: Automatic Metric for Reliable Optimization and Evaluation of Machine Translation Systems. In *Proceedings of the Sixth Workshop on Statistical Machine Translation*, pages 85–91, Edinburgh, Scotland. ACL.

Doddington, G. (2002). Automatic Evaluation of Machine Translation Quality Using n-gram Co-occurrence Statistics. In *Proceedings of the Second International Conference on Human*

Language Technology Research, HLT '02, pages 138–145, San Francisco, CA, USA. Morgan Kaufmann Publishers Inc.

Federmann, C. (2012a). Can Machine Learning Algorithms Improve Phrase Selection in Hybrid Machine Translation? In *Proceedings of the Joint Workshop on Hybrid Approaches to Machine Translation (HyTra)*, pages 113–118, Avignon, France. European Chapter of the ACL (EACL).

Federmann, C. (2012b). Hybrid Machine Translation Using Joint, Binarised Feature Vectors. In *Proceedings of the Tenth Biennial Conference of the Association for Machine Translation in the Americas (AMTA 2012)*, pages 113–118, San Diego, USA. AMTA.

Federmann, C. (2012c). A Machine-Learning Framework for Hybrid Machine Translation. In *Proceedings of the 35th Annual German Conference on Artificial Intelligence (KI-2012)*, pages 37–48, Saarbrücken, Germany. Springer, Heidelberg.

Federmann, C. and Hunsicker, S. (2011). Stochastic Parse Tree Selection for an Existing RBMT System. In *Proceedings of the Sixth Workshop on Statistical Machine Translation*, pages 351–357, Edinburgh, Scotland. ACL.

Federmann, C., Theison, S., Eisele, A., Uszkoreit, H., Chen, Y., Jellinghaus, M., and Hunsicker, S. (2009). Translation Combination using Factored Word Substitution. In *Proceedings of the Fourth Workshop on Statistical Machine Translation*, pages 70–74, Athens, Greece. ACL.

Frederking, R. and Nirenburg, S. (1994). Three Heads are Better Than One. In *Proceedings of the Fourth Conference on Applied Natural Language Processing*, ANLC '94, pages 95–100, Stroudsburg, PA, USA. ACL.

Gamon, M., Aue, A., and Smets, M. (2005). Sentence-level MT Evaluation Without Reference Translations: Beyond Language Modeling. In *Proceedings of the 10th EAMT Conference "Practical applications of machine translation"*, pages 103–111. EAMT.

He, Y., Ma, Y., van Genabith, J., and Way, A. (2010). Bridging SMT and TM with Translation Recommendation. In *Proceedings of the 48th Annual Meeting of the ACL*, ACL '10, pages 622–630, Stroudsburg, PA, USA. ACL.

Hunsicker, S., Yu, C., and Federmann, C. (2012). Machine Learning for Hybrid Machine Translation. In *Proceedings of the Seventh Workshop on Statistical Machine Translation*, pages 312–316, Montréal, Canada. ACL.

Klein, D. and Manning, C. (2003). Accurate Unlexicalized Parsing. In *Proceedings of the 41st Meeting of the Association for Computational Linguistics*, volume 1 of *ACL '03*, pages 423–430, Stroudsburg, PA, USA. ACL.

Papineni, K., Roukos, S., Ward, T., and Zhu, W.-J. (2002). BLEU: A Method for Automatic Evaluation of Machine Translation. In *Proceedings of the 40th Annual Meeting of the Association for Computational Linguistics*, ACL '02, pages 311–318, Stroudsburg, PA, USA. ACL.

Rosti, A.-V., Ayan, N. F., Xiang, B., Matsoukas, S., Schwartz, R., and Dorr, B. (2007). Combining Outputs from Multiple Machine Translation Systems. In *HLT 2007: The Conference of the North American Chapter of the ACL*, pages 228–235, Rochester, New York. ACL.

Stolcke, A. (2002). SRILM - An Extensible Language Modeling Toolkit. In *Proceedings of the International Conference on Spoken Language Processing*, pages 257–286.

Results from the ML4HMT-12 Shared Task on Applying Machine Learning Techniques to Optimise the Division of Labour in Hybrid Machine Translation

Christian FEDERMANN[1] *Tsuyoshi OKITA*[2] *Maite MELERO*[3]
Marta R. COSTA−JUSSÀ[3] *Toni BADIA*[3] *Josef VAN GENABITH*[2]
(1) DFKI GmbH, Language Technology Lab, Stuhlsatzenhausweg 3, D-66123 Saarbrücken, GERMANY
(2) Dublin City University, School of Computing, Glasnevin, Dublin 9, IRELAND
(3) Barcelona Media, Speech and Language Group, Diagonal 177, 08018 Barcelona, SPAIN
cfedermann@dfki.de {tokita,josef}@computing.dcu.ie
{maite.melero,marta.ruiz,toni.badia}@barcelonamedia.org

Abstract

We describe the second edition of the ML4HMT shared task which challenges participants to create hybrid translations from the translation output of several individual MT systems. We provide an overview of the shared task and the data made available to participants before briefly describing the individual systems. We report on the results using automatic evaluation metrics and conclude with a summary of ML4HMT-12 and an outlook to future work.

Keywords: Machine Translation, System Combination, Machine Learning.

1 Introduction

The ML4HMT-12 workshop and associated shared task are an effort to trigger a systematic investigation on improving state-of-the-art hybrid machine translation, making use of advanced machine-learning (ML) methodologies. The first edition of the workshop (ML4HMT-11) also road-tested a shared task (and associated data set) described and summarised in (Federmann, 2011). The main focus of the ML4HMT-12 (and ML4HMT-11) shared task is to address the question:

> Can Hybrid MT and System Combination techniques benefit from extra information (linguistically motivated, decoding, runtime, confidence scores or other meta-data) from the individual MT systems involved?

Participants are invited to build hybrid MT systems and/or system combinations by using the output of several MT systems of different types, as provided by the organisers. While participants are encouraged to explore machine learning techniques to explore the additional meta-data information sources, other approaches aimed at general improvements in hybrid and combination based MT are welcome to participate in the challenge. For systems that exploit additional meta-data information the challenge is that additional meta-data is highly heterogeneous and specific to individual systems.

One of the core objectives of the challenge is to build an MT combination (or more generally a hybrid MT) mechanism, where possible making effective use of the system-specific MT meta-data output produced by the participating individual MT systems as provided by the challenge development set data comprising outputs of four distinct MT systems and various meta-data annotations. The development set provided by the organisers can be used for tuning the combination or hybrid systems during the development phase.

2 Datasets

The organisers of the ML4HMT-12 shared task provide two data sets, one for the language pair Spanish→English (ES-EN), the other for Chinese→English (ZH-EN).

ES-EN Participants are given a development bilingual data set aligned at a sentence level. Each "bilingual sentence" contains:

1. the source sentence;
2. the target (reference) sentence; and
3. the corresponding translations from four individual component MT systems, based on different machine translation paradigms (Apertium (Ramírez-Sánchez et al., 2006); Lucy (Alonso and Thurmair, 2003); two different variants of Moses (Koehn et al., 2007): PB-SMT and HPB-SMT).

The output has been automatically annotated with system-internal meta-data information derived from the translation process of each of the systems.

ZH-EN A corresponding data set for Chinese→English with output translations from three systems (Moses; ICT_Chiero (Mi et al., 2009); Huajian RBMT) was prepared. Again, system output has been automatically annotated with system-internal meta-data information.

In total, with the development data participants received 20,000 translations per system for training and had to translate a test set containing 3,003 sentences ("newstest2011") for Spanish→English, while for the other language pair Chinese→English, a total of 6,752 training sentences per system were available while the test set had a size of 1,357 sentences.

3 Participants

We received six submissions for the Spanish→English translation task and none for Chinese→English. Below, we will briefly describe the participating systems.

3.1 DCU-Alignment

The authors of (Wu et al., 2012) incorporate alignment information as additional meta-data into their system combination module which does not originally utilise any alignment information provided by the individual MT systems producing the candidate translations. The authors add alignment information provided by one of the MT systems, the Lucy RBMT engine, into the internal, monolingual, alignment process. Unfortunately, the extracted alignment is often already a subset of alignments calculated by the monolingual aligner in the system combination and hence the approach does not augment the overall system combination performance as much as expected.

3.2 DCU-QE1

The submission described in (Okita et al., 2012a) incorporates a sentence-level Quality Estimation (QE) score as meta-data into their system combination module. Recently, QE or confidence estimation technology has advanced. It measures the quality of translations without references. The core idea is to incorporate this knowledge into the system combination module through an improved backbone selection.

3.3 DCU-QE2

The work described in (Okita et al., 2012a) also explains how one can incorporate a sentence-level Quality Estimation score to do the data selection process. The authors designed, hence, a method only based on Machine Learning. The translated output tends to preserve the translation quality as is expected, which results in a high Meteor score. The idea in this paper is to select one of the given translation outputs by QE score where a sentence-level QE technology is to measure the confidence estimation for the translation output.

3.4 DCU-DA

The authors of (Okita et al., 2012b) utilised unsupervised topic/genre classification results as meta-data, feeding into their system combination module. Since this module has access to topic/genre information, an MT system can take advantage of this information. MT systems are tuned to particular topic/genre groups and only compute translations for documents in this group, hence the performance of such MT systems may improve.

3.5 DCU-LM

This submission incorporates latent variables as meta-data into the system combination module. Information about those latent variables are supplied by a probabilistic neural language model. This language model can be trained on a huge monolingual corpus, with the disadvantage that the training of such a model takes considerable time. In fact, the LM used for ML4HMT-12 was small due to the huge cost of training, resulting in only small performance gains.

	Spanish→English					
Score	1best	R3	DCU-DA	DCU-LM	DCU-QE1	DFKI
Meteor	0.30692	0.32226	0.32124	0.31684	0.31712	**0.32303**
NIST	7.4296	7.4291	**7.6771**	7.5642	7.6481	7.2830
BLEU	0.2614	0.2524	**0.2634**	0.2562	0.2587	0.2570

Table 1: Translation quality of ML4HMT-12 submissions measured using Meteor, NIST, and BLEU scores for language pair Spanish→English. Best system per metric printed in bold face.

3.6 DFKI

This submission implements a method for system combination based on joint, binarised feature vectors as introduced in (Federmann, 2012b). It can be used to combine several black-box source systems. The authors first define a total order on the given translation output which can be used to partition an n-best list of translations into a set of pairwise system comparisons. Using this data, they train an SVM-based classification model and show how this classifier can be applied to combine translation output on the sentence level.

4 Results

Similar to the first edition of the ML4HMT shared task (ML4HMT-11), we aim to run both an automatic and a manual evaluation campaign. We consider three automatic scoring metrics, namely Meteor (Denkowski and Lavie, 2011), NIST (Doddington, 2002), and BLEU (Papineni et al., 2002), which are all well-renowned evaluation metrics commonly used for MT evaluation. Manual evaluation is currently being conducted using the Appraise software toolkit as described in (Federmann, 2012a). Table 1 summarises the results for all participating systems.

5 Conclusion

System *DFKI* performed best in terms of Meteor score[1] while system *DCU-DA* achieved best performance for NIST and BLEU scores. It will be interesting to see how these findings correlate with the results from manual evaluation, something we will report on in future work.

If technically feasible, we also intend to apply the algorithms submitted to the Spanish→English portion of the Shared Task to the second language pair, Chinese→English.

Acknowledgments

This work has been supported by the Seventh Framework Programme for Research and Technological Development of the European Commission through the T4ME contract (grant agreement: 249119) as well as by Science Foundation Ireland (Grant No. 07/CE/I1142) as part of the Centre for Next Generation Localisation (`http://www.cngl.ie/`) at Dublin City University. We are grateful to the organisers of COLING for supporting ML4HMT-12. Also, we are greatly indebted to all members of our program committee for their excellent and timely reviewing work and useful comments and feedback. Last but not least we want to express our sincere gratitude to all participants of the shared task for their interesting submissions.

[1] Which, in the first edition of the ML4HMT shared task, had shown the best correlation with human judgments. A finding that will be investigated in more detail once results from the manual evaluation of ML4HMT-12 are available.

References

Alonso, J. A. and Thurmair, G. (2003). The Comprendium Translator system. In *Proceedings of the Ninth Machine Translation Summit*, New Orleans, USA.

Denkowski, M. and Lavie, A. (2011). Meteor 1.3: Automatic Metric for Reliable Optimization and Evaluation of Machine Translation Systems. In *Proceedings of the Sixth Workshop on Statistical Machine Translation*, pages 85–91, Edinburgh, Scotland. ACL.

Doddington, G. (2002). Automatic Evaluation of Machine Translation Quality Using n-gram Co-occurrence Statistics. In *Proceedings of the Second International Conference on Human Language Technology Research*, HLT '02, pages 138–145, San Francisco, CA, USA. Morgan Kaufmann Publishers Inc.

Federmann, C. (2011). Results from the ML4HMT Shared Task on Applying Machine Learning Techniques to Optimise the Division of Labour in Hybrid Machine Translation. In *Proceedings of the International Workshop on Using Linguistic Information for Hybrid Machine Translation (LIHMT 2011) and of the Shared Task on Applying Machine Learning Techniques to Optimise the Division of Labour in Hybrid Machine Translation (ML4. Shared Task on Applying Machine Learning Techniques to Optimise the Division of Labour in Hybrid Machine Translation (ML4HMT-11)*, pages 110–117, Barcelona, Spain. META-NET.

Federmann, C. (2012a). Appraise: An Open-Source Toolkit for Manual Evaluation of Machine Translation Output. *The Prague Bulletin of Mathematical Linguistics (PBML)*, 98:25–35.

Federmann, C. (2012b). A Machine-Learning Framework for Hybrid Machine Translation. In *Proceedings of the 35th Annual German Conference on Artificial Intelligence (KI-2012)*, pages 37–48, Saarbrücken, Germany. Springer, Heidelberg.

Koehn, P., Hoang, H., Birch, A., Callison-Burch, C., Federico, M., Bertoldi, N., Cowan, B., Shen, W., Moran, C., Zens, R., Dyer, C., Bojar, O., Constantin, A., and Herbst, E. (2007). Moses: Open Source Toolkit for Statistical Machine Translation. In *Proceedings of ACL Demo and Poster Sessions*, pages 177–180. ACL.

Mi, H., Liu, Y., Xia, T., Xiao, X., Feng, Y., Xie, J., Xiong, H., Tu, Z., Zheng, D., Lu, Y., and Liu, Q. (2009). The ICT Statistical Machine Translation Systems for the IWSLT 2009. In *Proceedings of the International Workshop on Spoken Language Translation*, pages 55–59, Tokyo, Japan.

Okita, T., Rubino, R., and van Genabith, J. (2012a). Sentence-level quality estimation for mt system combination. In *Proceedings of the Second Shared Task on Applying Machine Learning Techniques to Optimise the Division of Labour in Hybrid Machine Translation (ML4HMT-12)*, Mumbai, India. Accepted for publication.

Okita, T., Toral, A., and van Genabith, J. (2012b). Topic modeling-based domain adaptation for system combination. In *Proceedings of the Second Shared Task on Applying Machine Learning Techniques to Optimise the Division of Labour in Hybrid Machine Translation (ML4HMT-12)*, Mumbai, India. Accepted for publication.

Papineni, K., Roukos, S., Ward, T., and Zhu, W.-J. (2002). BLEU: A Method for Automatic Evaluation of Machine Translation. In *Proceedings of the 40th Annual Meeting of the Association for Computational Linguistics*, ACL '02, pages 311–318, Stroudsburg, PA, USA. ACL.

Ramírez-Sánchez, G., Sánchez-Martínez, F., Ortiz-Rojas, S., Pérez-Ortiz, J. A., and Forcada, M. L. (2006). Opentrad apertium open-source machine translation system: an opportunity for business and research. In *Proceeding of Translating and the Computer 28 Conference*.

Wu, X., Okita, T., van Genabith, J., and Liu, Q. (2012). System combination with extra alignment information. In *Proceedings of the Second Shared Task on Applying Machine Learning Techniques to Optimise the Division of Labour in Hybrid Machine Translation (ML4HMT-12)*, Mumbai, India. Accepted for publication.

Author Index

Association for Computational Linguistics
209 N. Eighth Street
Stroudsburg, Pennsylvania 18360

CURRAN ASSOCIATES INC
proceedings.com